24-Hour Quilts

by Rita Weiss

Sterling Publishing Co., Inc.
New York

Library of Congress Cataloging-in-Publication Data
Weiss, Rita
   24-hour quilts / Rita Weiss
       p.   cm.
   ISBN 1-4027-1376-2
       1. Patchwork—Patterns. 2. Quilting. 3. Patchwork
quilts. I. Title: Twenty-four-hour quilts. II. Title.

TT835.W4496 2004
746.46'041—dc22   2004056590

              2   4   6   8   10   9   7   5   3

Published in paperback in 2006 by Sterling Publishing Co., Inc.
387 Park Avenue South, New York, NY 10016
© 2005 by The Creative Partners, LLC™
Distributed in Canada by Sterling Publishing
c/o Canadian Manda Group, 165 Dufferin Street
Toronto, Ontario, Canada M6K 3H6
Distributed in the United Kingdom by GMC Distribution Services,
Castle Place, 166 High Street, Lewes, East Sussex, England BN7 1XU
Distributed in Australia by Capricorn Link (Australia) Pty. Ltd.
P.O. Box 704, Windsor, NSW 2756, Australia

Sterling ISBN-13: 978-1-4027-1376-7 (Hardcover)
ISBN-10: 1-4027-1376-2

ISBN-13: 978-1-4027-3451-9 (Paperback)
ISBN-10: 1-4027-3451-4

For information about custom editions, special sales, premium and
corporate purchases, please contact Sterling Special Sales
Department at 800-805-5489 or specialsales@sterlingpub.com.

Introduction

I stayed away from quilting for many years. Too big a project: all that cutting and piecing and sewing back together by hand was discouraging.

Eureka! I discovered the sewing machine, and it started to come together. The real breakthrough, however, was the rotary cutter, which enabled quilters to cut through fabric quickly and accurately. Soon many of my quilting friends were teaching me techniques for quilting on the fast track; I became a quilter.

Quilting became a race. How fast could I actually make a quilt from start to finish. I set a goal for myself: to create a lovely quilt in under 24 hours. My pile of finished quilts got larger and larger; friends learned to accept a quilt from me for every occasion.

In this book, I share with you some of my favorite 24-hours quilts — actually my "Less-than-24-Hour-Quilts." There's not one quilt in this collection that takes more than 18 hours; some as few as six or seven hours. My dear friend Elsie Kirch helped to prepare the quilts for this book along with a group of dedicated quilters including: Faith Horsky, Erica Jarrett, C.J. McAuliffe, Val Shields, Kerry Smith,and Glenda Tucker. Most of the fabric used in the quilts was supplied by the FreeSpirit® fabric company, and the batting is courtesy of Fairfield Processing.

With each quilt, you'll find the amount of time that it took my friends and me to finish that quilt. But it's not a race. Twenty-four hours can be eight days of working for three hours; three eight-hour days, or 24 days of working only one hour per day. Making a quilt shouldn't be a chore. If it takes more than 24 hours to finish one of these quilts, that's okay. There's no prize for the one who finishes first. So whether you can finish your quilt in the allotted time, or twice that time, the results will be the same: a wonderful quilt that you can be proud of.

Contents

Rainbow Zigzag
8

Ragged Pinwheels
10

Angel Fantasy
12

Fractured Pinwheels
22

Ribbons and Stars
24

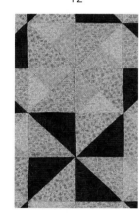

Stacked Pinwheels
26

Hug and Kiss
36

Oriental Garden
38

Corner Stars
40

Christmas Surprises
14

Musical Pinwheels
16

Patriotic Log Cabin
18

Floating Stars
20

Rosebuds
28

Shades of Blue
30

Log Cabin Garden Maze
32

Fiery Zigzag
34

Mini Floral Appliqué
42

Animal Checkerboard
44

Log Cabin Appliqué
46

Rainbow Zigzag

quilt is easy to piece using strip-piecing methods

If you have never made a quilt before, this is a great way to start. Although the quilt may be easy to piece using strip-piecing methods, the final results will proudly proclaim you as a quilter. The bright fabrics would make this a great quilt for a child. If you have been quilting for years, this quick quilt would be fun to squeeze in between your more elaborate and time-consuming projects.

INSTRUCTIONS APPEAR ON PAGE 50

Ragged Pinwheels

delightfully ragged appearance sure to appeal

Forget those lessons you learned at school about neatly constructing seams. In this quilt, two layers of flannel squares and triangles are sewn together with the seams showing on the front side of the quilt. The seam allowances are snipped; the quilt is dampened and put into the dryer. When the quilt is removed from the dryer it has a delightfully ragged appearance that is sure to appeal to the young and the young at heart.

INSTRUCTIONS APPEAR ON PAGE 53

Angel
Fantasy

If you believe in the power of angels, you will want to make this heavenly quilt which is fashioned from angel novelty prints surrounded by coordinating fabrics. If angels galvanize your imagination, then you probably have a stash of angel fabric; if not, use these instructions to create a quilt using a different theme for the novelty print squares. Two different nine-patch floral print blocks make the perfect setting for this pretty quilt that will enhance any room.

INSTRUCTIONS APPEAR ON PAGE 56

Christmas
Surprises

replete with Santas, snowmen, Christmas trees

Every year fabric companies present us with more and more wonderful Christmas novelty prints replete with Santas, snowmen, Christmas trees and more seasonal delights. Why not put a number of your favorites into a Christmas quilt that can be used to add a decorative note to your home. And, since Christmas is the time for surprises, be sure to add surprises in your quilt. If you follow the plan for this quilt, your surprise could be the red and green stars that will suddenly appear.

INSTRUCTIONS APPEAR ON PAGE 60

Musical Pinwheels

a quilt that will celebrate a love of music

If you are a music lover – or if you know a music lover – fabrics with the names and pictures of musical instruments certainly have a special warming message. They literally ask you to use them in a quilt that will celebrate a love of music. Add black and gold accent fabrics, follow the step-by-step instructions, and the resulting quilt will perform the perfect song on key.

INSTRUCTIONS APPEAR ON PAGE 64

Patriotic
Log Cabin

adding strips in numerical order to a center square

Who hasn't seen or even owned a Log Cabin quilt at one time or another? Probably the most popular of quilt patterns, Log Cabin quilt blocks are traditionally made by adding strips in numerical order to a center square. The center square in this quilt is made by fussy cutting flags from a patriotic fabric. Following the plan, red and blue logs are placed around this center square. What a great way to decorate your house on July 4th, or any other red, white and blue day.

INSTRUCTIONS APPEAR ON PAGE 68

18

Floating Stars

stars float and also assume many other shapes

Who doesn't find stars attractive? We find them in our songs, paintings, poetry, and – of course – in our flag. These stars seem not only to float in this quilt, but they also assume many other shapes and relationships, giving the finished design an Op Art look. In addition to the stars, diamonds appear when the star blocks are sewn together. Creating this quilt appears complicated, but it is constructed very simply from strips and squares.

INSTRUCTIONS APPEAR ON PAGE 72

Fractured Pinwheels

you'll be the only one who knows how easy it was

At first glance, this appears to be a very complicated quilt – all of those menacing triangles moving in opposite directions spell trouble. But, don't be dismayed. It's not a geometry lesson gone wrong. The pinwheel blocks are made by cutting pairs of strips diagonally and then re-sewing the light and dark triangles together. You'll be the only one who knows how easy it was to create this quilt leaving everyone else in awe.

INSTRUCTIONS APPEAR ON PAGE 75

Ribbons
and Stars

Your friends will be as astonished as was the neighborhood cat by the beauty of this quilt. The yellow stars seem to float in and out among the ribbons of green and burgundy. Made entirely with easy to cut and piece squares and half square triangles, the quilt is actually simple to create but especially striking in the effective use of color.

INSTRUCTIONS APPEAR ON PAGE 78

Stacked Pinwheels

Are you prepared for a mind-boggling experience? Pinwheels on top of pinwheels on top of pinwheels make for a phantasmagory of color and motion. The quilt is easy to construct as all of the shapes begin with squares that are cut diagonally in halves or quarters. The bright shades of pink, purple, blue, yellow and aqua give the quilt its added zip.

INSTRUCTIONS APPEAR ON PAGE 81

Rosebuds

an image of rosebuds dancing across the quilt

Bring the garden into the house! If you are a Log Cabin quilt fan, you will love this quilt because it is actually a version of the old faithful Log Cabin. Instead of making the quilt picture logs around a center red fireplace, these logs become leaves, and the centers are rosebuds. The leaves turn in every direction creating the image of the rosebuds dancing across the quilt. This garden is truly charming, filled with rosebuds of lavender, peach, pink and yellow.

INSTRUCTIONS APPEAR ON PAGE 84

Shades
of Blue

a magnificent composition that will enchant all

If you love the color blue, this is the quilt for you. Four different blue fabrics are combined with a little yellow and a little white to create the magnificent composition that will enchant all who see it. The blocks are made from one simple unit starting with a blue rectangle and a white or yellow square. Stars magically appear when the blocks are sewn together. If blue is not your favorite, try shades of red, or green — or whatever color suits your fancy.

INSTRUCTIONS APPEAR ON PAGE 88

Log Cabin
Garden Maze

if zigzagging through a maze is your thing

If strolling down a garden path and zigzagging through a maze is your thing, then search no further than the feeling in this quilt. Look closely; the quilt is actually a Log Cabin quilt made with logs of two different sizes. What a lovely and stately addition to any room.

INSTRUCTIONS APPEAR ON PAGE 92

Fiery Zigzag

The placement of red, orange and yellow fabric triangles makes this quilt look like a fiery zigzagging blaze. The quilt is shown tied rather than quilted making it a very quick project. If you prefer, you may want to quilt along the zigzags.

INSTRUCTIONS APPEAR ON PAGE 96

34

Hug and Kiss

a true "love you" quilt with a hidden message

Make this quilt for someone you love because it proclaims that you are sending hugs and kisses. When the blocks are turned and sewn together, they form "X" and "O" (the code for hugs and kisses). The quilt may look complicated to make, but upon closer examination, you will see that it is made up of simple four patches and half square triangles. A true "love you" quilt with a hidden message.

INSTRUCTIONS APPEAR ON PAGE 100

Oriental Garden

Four Patches and Strip blocks surrounding Japanese floral fabric squares capture the tranquility so reminiscent of the stillness of a Japanese garden. It is simple to construct, but the results will be a quilt that will inspire a mood of deep contemplation and meditation.

INSTRUCTIONS APPEAR ON PAGE 104

Corner Stars

hang on a wall like a fine modern painting

This is a quilt that you will certainly want to hang on a wall as if it were a fine modern painting. The construction of this clever quilt is so quick and simple that you'll be able to complete it in record time and enjoy it for a lifetime. It's made of half-square triangles of various colors that are sewn together creating stars.

INSTRUCTIONS APPEAR ON PAGE 107

Mini Floral
Appliqué

a quick gift that shows off your quilting prowess

If you need a quick gift and want to show off your quilting prowess, cut out flowers and leaves from a large floral print and fuse them to background fabric. Place batting behind the quilt top and then appliqué and quilt at the same time. These flowers come from the floral fabric line by Valori Wells for FreeSpirit Fabrics.

INSTRUCTIONS APPEAR ON PAGE 110

Animal
Checkerboard

No one can resist a new baby, and, of course, who can resist wanting to make a quilt for the new baby. Cute and coordinating baby animal fabrics, which are showcased in this charming quilt, will delight the new baby as well as the new mother. Because the quilt is tied, it can be finished in no time at all. If the new baby is a little boy, you might want to make his animal checkerboard out of blue fabrics.

INSTRUCTIONS APPEAR ON PAGE 112

44

Log Cabin
Appliqué

a simple log cabin with an easy appliquéd motif

This clever quilt combines a simple Log Cabin block with an easy appliquéd motif. The quilt is quick and easy because the appliqué pieces are fused onto the blocks and then quilted at the same time. No one will believe that it is so easy to finish. Its very simplicity adds to its attractiveness.

INSTRUCTIONS APPEAR ON PAGE 115

Quilt Patterns

Rainbow Zigzag Instructions

Approximate size: 60" x 72"
Block size: 12" finished
Approximate time: 7 hours

MATERIALS
1¹/₈ yds blue
³/₄ yd green
¹/₂ yd aqua
³/₄ yd orange
¹/₂ yd red
¹/₂ yd first border fabric
1 yd second border fabric
⁵/₈ yd binding fabric
3¹/₂ yds backing fabric
batting

CUTTING
Eight 4¹/₂"-wide strips, blue
Five 4¹/₂"-wide strips, green
Three 4¹/₂"-wide strips, aqua
Five 4¹/₂"-wide strips, orange
Three 4¹/₂"-wide strips, red
Six 2¹/₂"-wide strips, first border
Seven 4¹/₂"-wide strips, second border
Seven 2¹/₂"-wide strips, binding

INSTRUCTIONS

Making the Nine Patch

1. Cut two blue, one green, one aqua, one orange and one red strip in half so you have two shorter strips about $4\frac{1}{2}$" x 20". Set aside.

2. For row 1, sew blue, green and aqua strips together; repeat. Press seams to the right.

row 1

3. For row 2, sew orange, blue and green strips together; repeat. Press seams to the left.

row 2

4. For row 3, sew red, orange and blue strips together; repeat. Press seams to the right.

row 3

5. Repeat steps 2 to 4 with the $4\frac{1}{2}$" x 20" strips. You will now have $2\frac{1}{2}$ sets of strips for each row.

6. Cut each strip set into $4\frac{1}{2}$" pieces. You will need 20 pieces for each row.

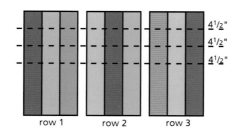

row 1   row 2   row 3

7. Sew rows together to complete Nine Patch.

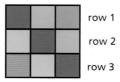

row 1
row 2
row 3

8. Make 20 Nine Patch blocks.

(continued on next page)

Quilt Layout

Making the Quilt Top

1. Place blocks referring to the layout. Sew the blocks together in rows, then sew rows together.

2. Refer to Adding the Borders on page 125 to add first and second borders to your quilt top.

3. Complete your quilt referring to the finishing instructions on pages 125 to 128.

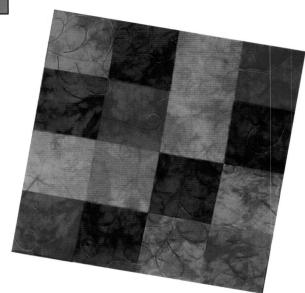

Ragged Pinwheels Instructions

Approximate size: 79" x 100"
Block size: 21" finished
Approximate time: 18 hours

MATERIALS

¾ yd dark blue flannel print
1⅝ yds yellow flannel print
1⅝ yds white flannel print
1⅝ yds medium blue flannel print
1⅝ yds medium aqua flannel print
1¼ yds first border flannel print
1¾ yds second border flannel print
11 yds backing

CUTTING

Twelve 8" x 8" squares, dark blue print
Twenty-four 9" x 9" squares,
    yellow print
Twenty-four 9" x 9" squares, white print
Twenty-four 9" x 9" squares,
    medium blue print
Twenty-four 9" x 9" squares,
    medium aqua print
Eight 4"-wide strips, first border print
Nine 6"-wide strips, second border print
Twelve 8" x 8" squares, backing fabric
Ninety-six 9" x 9" squares, backing fabric
Eight 4"-wide strips, backing fabric
Nine 6"-wide strips, backing fabric

INSTRUCTIONS

Notes: Sewing is done with a ¾" seam allowance along diagonal edges and a ½" seam allowance along all remaining edges. The seam allowances will be on the front of the quilt. Use a walking foot for easier sewing.

Making Pinwheel Block A

1. Place all 8" dark blue squares wrong sides together with an 8" backing fabric square; set aside. Treat each pair of squares as a single square during the construction process.

2. Place all yellow, white, medium blue and medium aqua 9" squares wrong sides together with 9" backing fabric squares. Treat each pair of squares as a single square during the construction process.

3. Draw a light diagonal pencil line on right side of each white and yellow square pair.

4. For Pinwheel A, place yellow square and medium blue square with backing sides together; sew ¾" from each side of drawn line.

5. Cut along drawn line for two triangle squares. Repeat for another pair of triangle squares.

6. Repeat steps 4 and 5 with white and medium blue squares.

7. Sew yellow/medium blue triangle squares, white/medium blue triangle squares and dark blue 8" square together to make Pinwheel A. Remember to sew with a ½" seam allowance, placing backing sides together.

8. Make six Pinwheel Block A.

9. Clip seam allowances close to seam every ½" to 1"

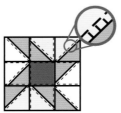

Making Pinwheel Block B

1. Repeat steps for Making Pinwheel Block A using medium aqua print in place of medium blue.

2. Make six Pinwheel Block B.

Making the Quilt Top

1. Place Pinwheel Block A and Pinwheel Block B according to layout. Sew blocks together in rows with backing sides together and a ½" seam allowance. Press seams for rows in alternating directions. Sew rows together. Press quilt top carefully.

2. Refer to Adding the Borders on page 125 to add first and second borders to your quilt top. **Note:** Piece border strips for front and back of quilt to desired length with right sides together. Once correct length is achieved, place front border strips and backing border strips with wrong sides together and attach to quilt with backing sides together and using a ½" seam allowance.

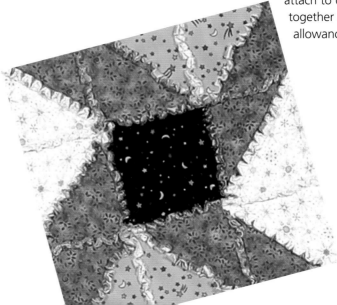

Quilt Layout

3. When both borders have been attached, sew ½" from outside edge of quilt (see diagram to right).

4. Clip all remaining seam allowances including outside edge.

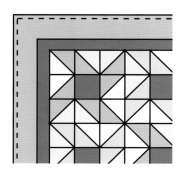

5. Dampen quilt and place in dryer. Repeat two or three times until clipped edges are fluffy.

Angel Fantasy Instructions

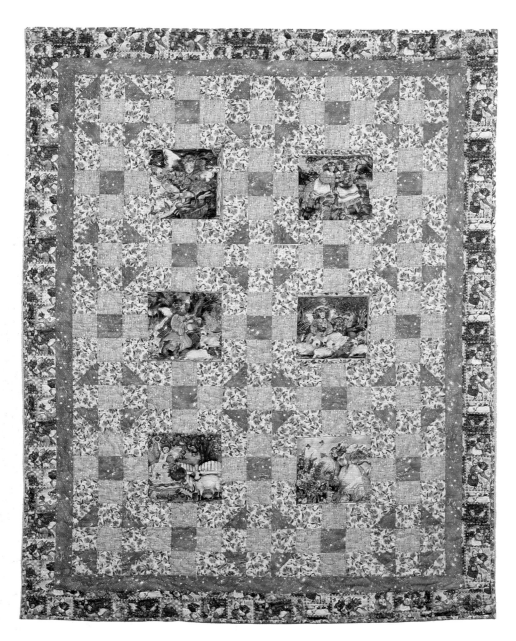

Approximate size: 57" x 75"
Block size: 9" finished
Approximate time: 8 hours

MATERIALS

Six angel novelty print squares,
   9½" x 9½" or ⅝ yd print fabric
1⅜ yds pink print
1½ yds blue floral
¾ yd blue star print
1 yd pink floral
⅝ yd first border print
1⅛ yds second border print
⅝ yd binding fabric
3½ yds backing fabric
batting

CUTTING

Six 9½" x 9½" squares,
   angel novelty print
Twelve 3½"-wide strips, pink print
Eight 3½"-wide strips, blue floral
   Cut two strips into 24 squares,
   3½" x 3½"
Three 4"-wide strips, blue floral
   Cut into 24 squares, 4" x 4"
Three 4"-wide strips, blue star print
   Cut into 24 squares, 4" x 4"
Two 3½"-wide strips, blue star print
Eight 3½"-wide strips, pink floral
Seven 2½"-wide strips, first border print
Eight 4½"-wide strips, second border print
Eight 2½"-wide strips, binding fabric

INSTRUCTIONS

Making Nine Patch A

1. Draw a light pencil line diagonally on wrong side of blue floral print squares.

2. Place a 4" blue floral square right sides together with a 4" blue star print square; sew ¼" from each side of drawn line.

3. Cut along drawn line for two triangle squares. Trim square to 3½" x 3½"; press seam to one side.

4. Repeat steps 2 and 3 for 48 triangle squares.

5. Sew a triangle square to each side of a 3½" blue floral square for rows 1 and 3.

rows 1 & 3

Press seams toward blue floral.

6. Sew a blue floral strip to each side of a pink print strip; repeat.

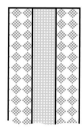

7. Cut strip sets every 3½" until you have twelve strips for row 2. Press seams toward blue floral.

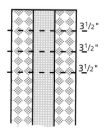
3½"
3½"
3½"

8. Sew rows 1, 2 and 3 together.

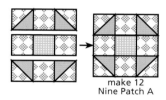
make 12
Nine Patch A

9. Make twelve Nine Patch blocks.

Making Nine Patch B

1. Sew a pink floral strip to each side of a pink print strip. Press seams toward pink print.

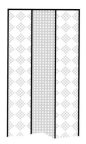

(continued on next page)

2. Cut strip set every 3½" for rows 1 and 3.

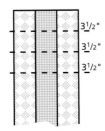

3. Sew a pink print strip to each side of a blue star print strip. Press seams toward pink print.

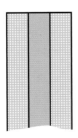

4. Cut strip set every 3½" for row 2.

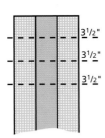

5. Sew rows 1, 2 and 3 together to complete Nine Patch B.

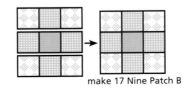

make 17 Nine Patch B

6. Make 17 Nine Patch B.

Making the Quilt Top

1. Place Nine Patch A blocks, Nine Patch B blocks and angel novelty print squares according to layout. Sew blocks together in rows. Press seams for rows in alternating directions. Sew rows together. Press quilt top carefully.

2. Refer to Adding the Borders on page 125 to add first and second borders to your quilt top.

3. Complete your quilt referring to the finishing instructions on pages 125 to 128.

Quilt Layout

Christmas Surprises Instructions

Approximate size: 36½" x 36½"
Block size: 6" finished
Approximate time: 6 hours

MATERIALS

1–1½ yds Christmas novelty print
½ yd red print (includes border)
½ yd green print (includes border)
¼ yd blue print
¼ yd gold
³/₈ yd binding fabric
1 yd backing fabric
batting

CUTTING

Sixteen 5" x 5" squares, novelty print
    (fussy cut individual motifs)
Three 2½"-wide strips, red print
    Cut into sixteen 2½" x 6" rectangles
Three 2½"-wide strips, green print
    Cut into sixteen 2½" x 6" rectangles
Four 1½"-wide strips, blue print
    (first border)
Four 1½"-wide strips, gold
    (second border)
Four 1½"-wide strips, green print
    (third border)
Eight 3½" squares, red print
    (corner squares)
Four 3½"-wide strips,
    Christmas novelty print (fourth border)
Four 2½"-wide strips, binding fabric

INSTRUCTIONS

Making the Blocks

1. Cut 16 red print rectangles and 16 green print rectangles in half diagonally.

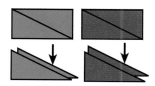

Note: Be sure to stack strips unfolded with right sides facing up. This will ensure that all triangles will face the same direction and not be mirror images.

These triangles are mirror images.

2. Sew diagonal edge of two red triangles to opposite sides of a Christmas novelty print square.

Note: Place wide end of triangle slightly above edge of square and sew with square on top of triangle.

3. Press triangles open.

4. Sew green triangles to remaining sides in same manner.

5. Square up block being sure to leave ¼" seam allowance beyond corners of center squares.

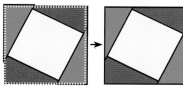

Trim to 1/4" from corners of center square.

6. Repeat steps 2 to 5 for remaining squares. **Note:** If your novelty print squares are directional, you must position triangles differently for half of the blocks.

make 6   make 6

You will need eight of each.

(continued on next page)

Making the Quilt Top

1. Place blocks in four rows of four blocks noting placement of triangles in the quilt layout. Sew the blocks together in rows. Press seams for rows in alternating directions. Sew rows together. Press quilt top carefully.

2. Sew the blue, gold and green 1½"-wide strips together. Press seams to one side. Make four strip sets.

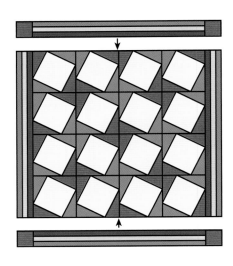

4. Sew a strip set to opposite sides of quilt. Sew 3½" square to ends of remaining two strip sets and sew to top and bottom of quilt.

3. Measure quilt top lengthwise and crosswise; both measurements should be 24½".

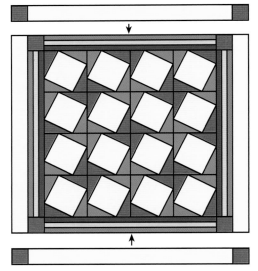

5. Repeat steps 3 and 4 with Christmas novelty print strips and red print squares.

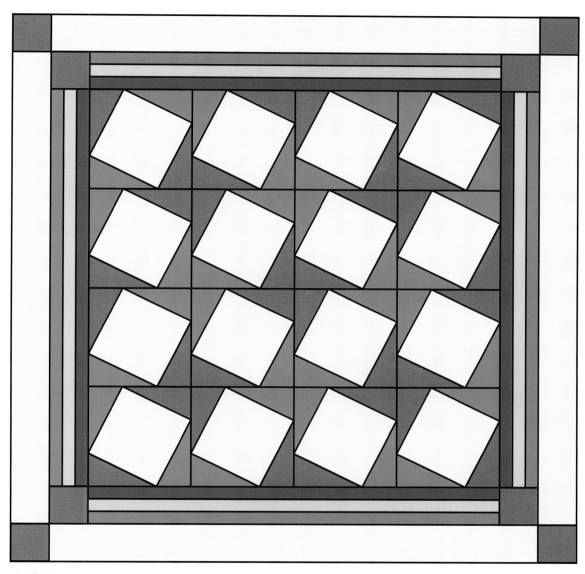

Quilt Layout

6. Complete your quilt referring to the finishing instructions on pages 125 to 128.

Musical Pinwheels Instructions

Approximate size: 49" x 57"
Block size: 8" finished
Approximate time: 7 hours

MATERIALS

⅝ yd black print 1
⅝ yd white musical print 1
⅝ yd black print 2
⅝ yd white musical print 2
¾ yd gold (includes border corners)
⅜ yd first border fabric
¼ yd second border fabric
⅝ yd third border print
⅝ yd binding fabric
3½ yds backing fabric
batting

CUTTING

Seven 2½"-wide strips, black print 1
Seven 2½"-wide strips,
   white musical print 1
Seven 2½"-wide strips, black print 2
Seven 2½"-wide strips,
   white musical print 2
Eight 2½"-wide strips, gold
   Cut into 120 squares, 2½" x 2½"
Five 2"-wide strips, first border
Five 1"-wide strips, second border
Six 3"-wide strips, third border print
Four 5" squares, gold (corner square)
Six 2½"-wide strips, binding fabric

INSTRUCTIONS

Making the Pinwheel Blocks

1. Sew black print 1 and white musical print 1 strips together. Press seams toward black print. You will have seven strip sets.

2. Sew black print 2 and white musical print 2 strips together. Press seams toward black print. You will have seven strip sets.

3. Cut strip sets every 4½" until you have 60 strip squares of black print 1/white musical print 1 and 60 squares of black print 2/white musical print 2.

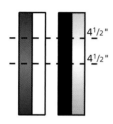

4. Place gold square right sides together with strip square, noting position.

5. Sew diagonally from corner to corner of gold square.

Hint: If you need a sewing guide, draw a light pencil line diagonally on wrong side of each gold square.

6. Trim diagonal seam about ¼" from seam, flip resulting triangle over and press.

7. Repeat steps 4 to 6 for all pieced squares making sure placement of gold square is the same on each.

8. For Pinwheel Block A, sew black print 1/white musical print 1 squares together in pairs, then sew pairs together. You will need 15 Pinwheel Block A.

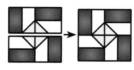

(continued on next page)

9. For Pinwheel Block B, sew black print 2/white musical print 2 squares together in pairs, then sew pairs together. You will need 15 Pinwheel Block B.

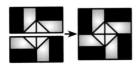

Making the Quilt Top

1. Place Pinwheel blocks in six rows of five blocks referring to the quilt layout. Sew the blocks together in rows. Press seams for rows in alternating directions. Sew rows together. Press quilt top carefully.

2. Measure quilt top lengthwise. Piece and cut border strips 1, 2 and 3 to that size; sew together. Sew to sides of quilt top.

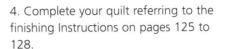

3. Measure quilt top crosswise. Piece and cut border strips 1, 2 and 3 to that size; sew together. Sew a 5" gold square at each end. Sew to top and bottom of quilt top.

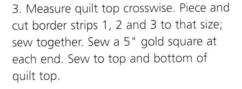

4. Complete your quilt referring to the finishing Instructions on pages 125 to 128.

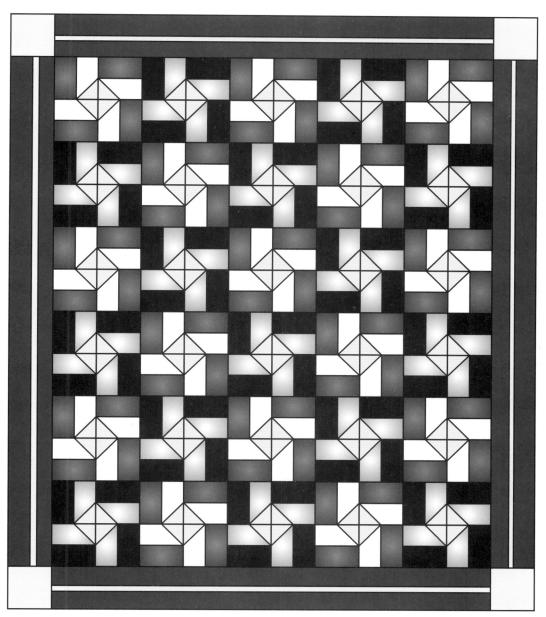

Quilt Layout

Patriotic Log Cabin Instructions

Approximate size: 35" x 43"
Block size: 8" finished
Approximate time: 6 hours

MATERIALS

½ yd patriotic novelty print
½ yd light blue
1 yd dark blue (includes second border)
1 yd red (includes first border)
½ yd binding fabric
1½ yds backing fabric
batting

CUTTING

Twenty-four 2½" squares, novelty print
  (fussy cut for center squares and
  border corners)
Twenty-two 1"-wide strips, red (logs 1–4,
  9–12)
Five 2½"-wide strips, light blue (logs 5, 6)
Seven 2½"-wide strips, dark blue
  (logs 7, 8)
Five 1"-wide strips, red (first border)
Six 2½"-wide strips, dark blue (second
  border)
Six 2½"-wide strips, binding

INSTRUCTIONS

Making the Log Cabin

Log Cabin blocks are constructed by adding strips in numerical order to a center square. There are two different ways to add the strips.

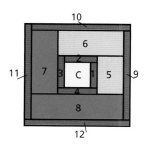

Method 1

1. Place red strip right sides together with the center square and sew with 1/4" seam allowance.

2. Fold strip over and finger press. Cut red strip even with center square.

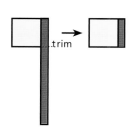

3. Turn clockwise, place red strip right sides together along right edge and sew. Fold strip over, finger press and cut red strip.

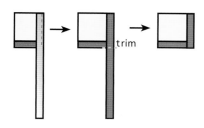

4. Turn clockwise again and add red strip in same manner.

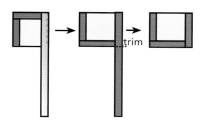

5. Continue adding strips in order until block is complete (see steps 1–9 below). Make 20 Log Cabin blocks.

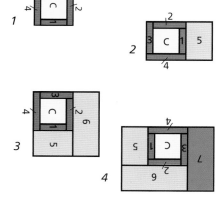

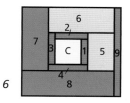

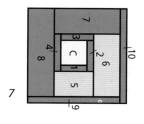

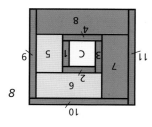

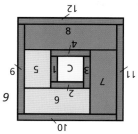

(continued on next page)

69

Method 2

1. Cut strips in the following amounts:

log 1 (red):
   twenty 1" x 2$\frac{1}{2}$" strips

logs 2, 3 (red):
   forty 1" x 3" strips

log 4 (red):
   twenty 1" x 3$\frac{1}{2}$" strips

log 5 (light blue):
   twenty 2$\frac{1}{2}$" x 3$\frac{1}{2}$" strips

log 6 (light blue):
   twenty 2$\frac{1}{2}$" x 5$\frac{1}{2}$" strips

log 7 (dark blue):
   twenty 2$\frac{1}{2}$" x 5$\frac{1}{2}$" strips

log 8 (dark blue):
   twenty 2$\frac{1}{2}$" x 7$\frac{1}{2}$" strips

log 9 (red):
   twenty 1" x 7$\frac{1}{2}$" strips

log 10, 11 (red):
   forty 1" x 8" strips

log 12 (red):
   twenty 1" x 8$\frac{1}{2}$" strips

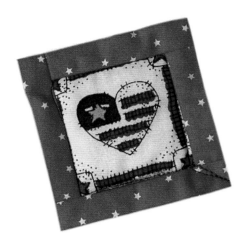

2. Sew log 1 to right edge of center square; finger press open.

3. Turn clockwise and sew log 2 to right edge; finger press open.

4. Turn clockwise and sew log 3 to right edge; finger press open.

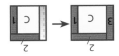

5. Continue sewing logs in numerical order until block is complete. Make 20 Log Cabin blocks.

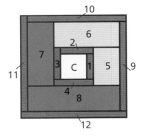

Making the Quilt Top

1. Place blocks in five rows of four blocks. Sew the blocks together in rows, Press seams for rows in alternating directions. Sew rows together.

2. Refer to Adding the Borders on page 125 to add first border. To add second border, measure length and width of quilt. Cut and sew two border strips to equal the length and two to equal the width. Sew border to sides of quilt first. Sew 2$\frac{1}{2}$" novelty print square to each end of remaining border strips. Sew to top and bottom of quilt.

3. Complete your quilt referring to the finishing instructions on pages 125 to 128.

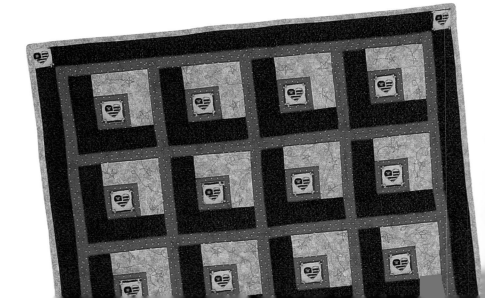

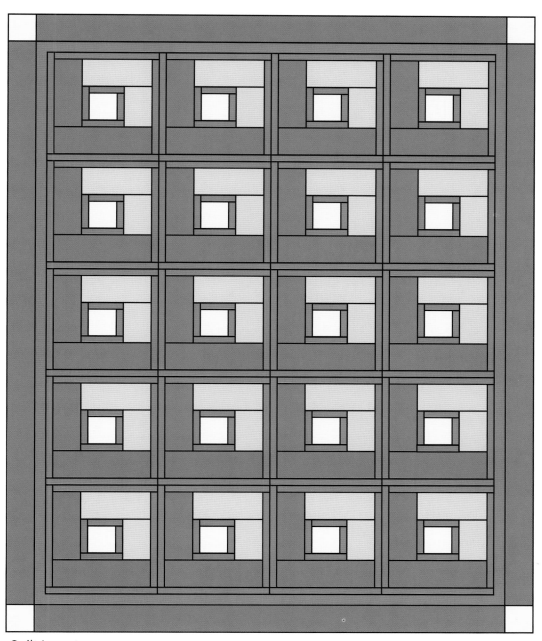

Quilt Layout

Floating Stars Instructions

Approximate size: 60" x 60"
Block size: 12" finished
Approximate time: 10 hours

MATERIALS

³/₄ yd dark blue
³/₄ yd burgundy
1¹/₄ yds gold
1 yd medium burgundy print
¹/₂ yd first border print
1 yd second border print
⁵/₈ yd binding fabric
3¹/₂ yds backing fabric
batting

CUTTING

Five 4"-wide strips, dark blue
   Cut into 48 squares, 4" x 4"
Three 3¹/₂"-wide strips, burgundy
   Cut into 32 squares, 3¹/₂" x 3¹/₂"
Two 4"-wide strips, burgundy
   Cut into 16 squares, 4" x 4"
Seven 4"-wide strips, gold
   Cut into 64 squares, 4" x 4"
Three 3¹/₂"-wide strips, gold
   Cut into 32 squares, 3¹/₂" x 3¹/₂"
Four 6⁷/₈"-wide strips, medium burgundy
   print
   Cut into 16 squares, 6⁷/₈" x 6⁷/₈"
Six 2"-wide strips, first border fabric
Seven 4"-wide strips, second border print
Seven 2¹/₂"-wide strips, binding fabric

INSTRUCTIONS

Making Unit A

1. Draw a diagonal line on wrong side of burgundy or dark blue squares (whichever are lighter in color).

2. Place burgundy and dark blue squares right sides together; sew 1/4" from each side of drawn line.

3. Cut along drawn line to get two triangle squares. Make 32 triangle squares.

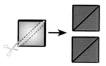

4. Trim triangle squares to 3 1/2" squares.

5. Cut 4" gold squares diagonally in half. Sew a gold triangle to adjacent (dark blue) sides of each triangle square. Press seams toward gold triangle. Trim diagonal edge to 1/4" from corner of triangle square. Short sides should measure 6 7/8".

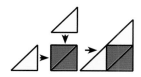

6. Cut 6 7/8" medium burgundy print triangles diagonally in half. Sew a triangle to unit made in step 5 to complete Unit A.

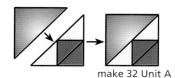

make 32 Unit A

7. Make 32 Unit A.

Making Unit B

1. Draw a diagonal line on wrong side of 4" gold squares. Place 4" gold squares right sides together with 4" dark blue squares; sew 1/4" from each side of drawn line.

2. Cut along drawn line for two triangle squares. Press seams toward dark blue fabric.

3. Sew triangle square to 3 1/2" gold square.

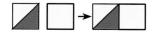

4. Sew triangle square to 3 1/2" burgundy square.

5. Sew units from steps 3 and 4 together to complete Unit B.

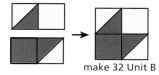

make 32 Unit B

6. Make 32 Unit B.

(continued on next page)

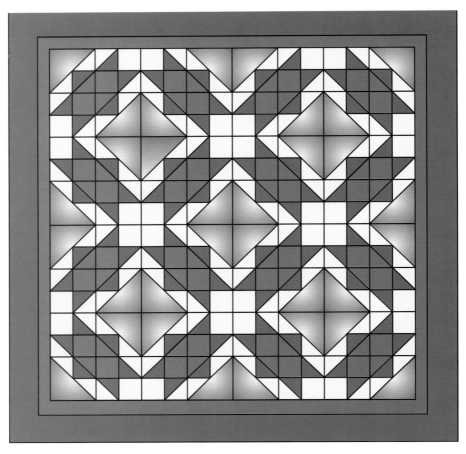

Quilt Layout

Making the Star Block

1. Sew a Unit A and Unit B together; repeat.

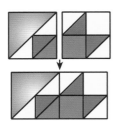

2. Sew units from step 1 together to complete block.

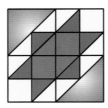

3. Make 16 Star Blocks.

Making the Quilt Top

1. Place blocks referring to the layout. Sew the blocks together in rows, Press seams for rows in alternating directions. Sew rows together.

2. Refer to Adding the Borders on page 125 to add first and second borders to your quilt top.

3. Complete your quilt referring to the finishing Instructions on pages 125 to 128.

Fractured Pinwheels Instructions

Approximate size: 42" x 53"
Block size: 11" finished
Approximate time: 5 hours

MATERIALS

½ yd dark pink
½ yd light pink
½ yd dark turquoise
½ yd light turquoise
⅜ yd first border fabric
¾ yd second border fabric
½ yd binding fabric
3½ yds backing fabric
batting

CUTTING

Four 3½"-wide strips, dark pink
Four 3½"-wide strips, light pink
Four 3½"- wide strips, dark turquoise
Four 3½"-wide strips, light turquoise
Five 2"-wide strips, first border
Six 3½"-wide strips, second border
Six 2½"-wide strips, binding

INSTRUCTIONS

Making the Pinwheel Block

1. Sew dark turquoise and dark pink strips together. Press seams toward dark turquoise. You will need four strip sets.

2. Sew light turquoise and light pink strips together. Press seams toward light pink. You will need four strip sets.

3. Cut strip sets every 6½" until you have 24 squares of each combination.

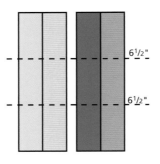

4. Cut each square diagonally in half. **Note:** You will have two different pieced triangles for each combination.

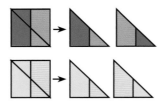

5. Sew a dark triangle to light triangle to make a pieced square; repeat for 24 squares of each combination. Trim squares to 6" square.

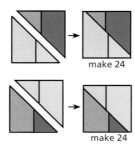

make 24

make 24

Hint: Place triangles to be sewn together with right sides together, stack next to sewing machine. Pick up two triangles and sew along diagonal edge. Continue chain piecing until all pairs are sewn together.

6. Take four like squares and sew in pairs, noting position; sew pairs together to form Pinwheel Block A. Repeat for five more blocks.

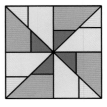

7. Repeat step 6 with the remaining pieced triangles to form 6 of Pinwheel Block B.

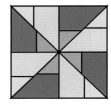

Making the Quilt Top

1. Place Pinwheel blocks in four rows of three blocks referring to the quilt layout. Sew the blocks together in rows. Press seams for rows in alternating directions. Sew rows together. Press quilt top carefully.

2. Refer to Adding the Borders on page 125 to add first and second borders to your quilt top.

3. Complete your quilt referring to the Finishing Instructions on pages 125 to 128.

Quilt Layout

Approximate size: 61" x 76"
Block size: 15" finished
Approximate time: 9 hours

MATERIALS

1¼ yds light yellow
⅞ yd light green
⅞ yd dark green
⅞ yd burgundy
⅝ yd first border print
1⅝ yds second border print
⅝ yd binding fabric
3½ yds backing fabric
batting

CUTTING

Two 5½"-wide strips, light yellow
    Cut into twelve squares, 5½" x 5½"
Four 6"-wide strips, light yellow
    Cut into 24 squares, 6" x 6"
Four 6"-wide strips, light green
    Cut into 24 squares, 6" x 6"
Four 6"-wide strips, dark green
    Cut into 24 squares, 6" x 6"
Four 6"-wide strips, burgundy
    Cut into 24 squares, 6" x 6"
Six 3"-wide strips, first border fabric
Seven 6"-wide strips, second border print
Seven 2½"-wide strips, binding fabric

INSTRUCTIONS

Making the Star Block

1. Draw a diagonal line on wrong side of light yellow and light green 6" squares.

2. Place light yellow square right sides together with burgundy square; sew ¼" from each side of diagonal line.

3. Cut along drawn line for two triangle squares. Trim to 5½" square. Make 24 triangle squares.

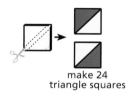

make 24
triangle squares

4. Repeat steps 2 and 3 with light yellow and dark green squares, light green and burgundy squares and light green and dark green squares. Trim to 5½" square.

make 24 triangle squares
of each combination

5. Sew triangle squares and 5½" light yellow square together in rows. Press seams for alternating rows in opposite directions. Sew rows together to complete Star Block.

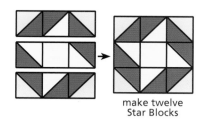

make twelve
Star Blocks

6. Make twelve Star Blocks.

(continued on next page)

Quilt Layout

Making the Quilt Top

1. Place blocks referring to the layout. Sew the blocks together in rows. Press seams for rows in alternating directions.

Sew rows together.

2. Refer to Adding the Borders on page 125 to add first and second borders to your quilt top.

3. Complete your quilt referring to the finishing instructions on pages 125 to 128.

Stacked Pinwheels Instructions

Approximate size: 50" x 60"
Block size: 10" finished
Approximate time: 7 hours

MATERIALS

⅝ yd pink
⅝ yd purple
⅝ yd dark blue
½ yd yellow
½ yd aqua
½ yd first border fabric
¾ yd second border fabric
3¼ yds backing fabric
⅝ yd binding fabric
batting

CUTTING

20 - 6" x 6" squares, pink
   Cut diagonally in half
20 - 6" x 6" squares, purple
   Cut diagonally in half
20 - 6" x 6" squares, dark blue
   Cut diagonally in half
Ten 6½" x 6½" squares, yellow
   Cut diagonally in quarters
Ten 6½" x 6½" squares, aqua
   Cut diagonally in quarters
Six 2"-wide strips, first border
Six 4"-wide strips, second border
Six 2½"-wide strips, binding

INSTRUCTIONS

Making the Pinwheel Blocks

1. Sew 20 pink triangles to 20 dark blue triangles; sew 20 purple triangles to 20 dark blue triangles. Press seams toward pink and purple triangles and trim squares to 5½" square. **Hint:** Use the 45-degree line on your acrylic ruler as a guide when trimming squares. This will ensure that your seam line goes from corner to corner.

make 20   make 20

2. Sew aqua and yellow triangles together.

make 40

Note: Be sure to always sew with the yellow triangle on top and from the wide end of the triangles toward the narrow end. Press seam to one side.

3. Sew yellow/aqua triangles to pink and purple triangles. Press toward pink and purple triangles. Trim squares to 5½".

make 20   make 20

4. For pink Pinwheel Block, sew dark blue/pink squares to squares from step 3; repeat.

Sew pairs of squares together to complete block. Make ten pink Pinwheel Blocks.

make 10

5. Repeat step 4 for ten purple Pinwheel Blocks.

make 10

Making the Quilt Top

1. Place blocks referring to the layout, alternating pink and purple Pinwheel blocks. Sew the blocks together in rows, press seams for rows in alternating directions. Sew rows together.

2. Refer to Adding the Borders on page 125 to add first and second borders to your quilt top.

3. Complete your quilt referring to the finishing instructions on pages 125 to 128.

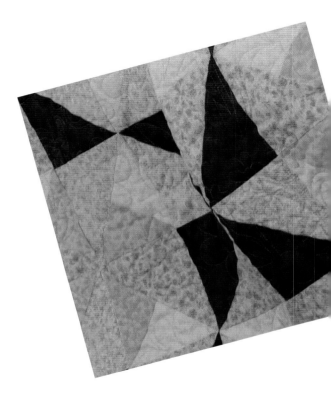

Quilt Layout

Rosebuds Instructions

Approximate size: 50" x 56"
Block size: 6" finished
Approximate time: 11 hours

MATERIALS

$\frac{1}{8}$ yd each lavender, peach,
  pink and yellow
$\frac{7}{8}$ yd light aqua floral
$\frac{3}{4}$ yd dark teal
$\frac{3}{4}$ yd medium dark teal
$\frac{5}{8}$ yd light aqua solid
$\frac{1}{2}$ yd first border print
1 yd second border print
$\frac{1}{2}$ yd binding fabric
$3\frac{1}{2}$ yds backing fabric
batting

CUTTING

14 - $2\frac{1}{2}$" squares each of yellow, peach,
  pink and lavender (center squares)
Ten $2\frac{1}{2}$"-wide strips, light aqua floral
  (logs 1, 2)
Eight $2\frac{1}{2}$"-wide strips, dark teal
  (logs 3, 4)
Eight $2\frac{1}{2}$"-wide strips, medium dark teal
  (logs 3, 4)
Seven $2\frac{1}{2}$"-wide strips, light aqua solid
  (corner triangles)
  Cut into 112 squares, $2\frac{1}{2}$" x $2\frac{1}{2}$"
Six 2"-wide strips, first border fabric
Seven 3"-wide strips, second border print
Seven $2\frac{1}{2}$"-wide strips, binding fabric

INSTRUCTIONS

Note: Half of the blocks are made with dark teal and half are made with medium dark teal.

Making the Rosebud Block

The Rosebud blocks are constructed like Log Cabin blocks by adding strips in numerical order to a center square. There are two different ways to add the strips.

Method 1

1. Place light aqua floral strip right sides together with the center square and sew with 1/4" seam allowance.

2. Fold strip over and finger press. Cut light aqua floral strip even with center square.

3. Turn counterclockwise, place light aqua strip right sides together along right edge and sew. Fold strip over, finger press and cut light aqua floral strip.

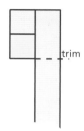

4. Turn counterclockwise again and add dark teal strip in same manner.

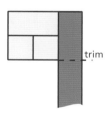

5. Turn counterclockwise again and add dark teal strip in same manner to compete Log Cabin block. Make 56 Log Cabin blocks. **Note:** There will be 14 blocks with pink centers, 14 with lavender, 14 with yellow and 14 with peach centers.

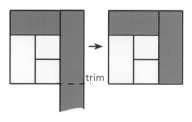

(continued on next page)

Method 2

1. Cut strips in the following amounts:

log 1 (light aqua floral):
    fifty-six - 2¹/₂" x 2¹/₂" strips

log 2 (light aqua floral):
    fifty-six - 2¹/₂" x 4¹/₂" strips

log 3 (dark teal):
    twenty-eight - 2¹/₂" x 4¹/₂" strips

log 3 (medium dark teal):
    twenty-eight - 2¹/₂" x 4¹/₂" strips

log 4 (dark teal):
    twenty-eight - 2¹/₂" x 6¹/₂" strips

log 4 (medium dark teal):
    twenty-eight - 2¹/₂" x 6¹/₂" strips

2. Sew log 1 to right edge of center square; finger press open.

3. Turn counterclockwise and sew log 2 to right edge; finger press open.

4. Turn counterclockwise and sew log 3 to right edge; finger press open.

5. Turn counterclockwise and sew log 4 to right edge; finger press open. Make 56 Log Cabin blocks. **Note:** There will be 14 blocks with pink centers, 14 with lavender, 14 with yellow and 14 with peach centers.

Finishing the Rosebud Block

1. Place a light aqua square right sides together with opposite dark teal (or medium dark teal) corners of Log Cabin block; sew diagonally from corner to corner of light aqua square.

Hint: Draw a light pencil line diagonally on wrong side of each square for a sewing guideline.

2. Trim corners about ¹/₄" from stitching.

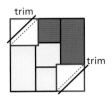

3. Press open resulting triangles to complete Rosebud block.

Rosebud Block

4. Make 56 Rosebud blocks.

Making the Quilt Top

1. Place blocks referring to the layout. Sew the blocks together in rows, Press seams for rows in alternating directions. Sew rows together.

2. Refer to Adding the Borders on page 125 to add first and second borders to your quilt top.

3. Complete your quilt referring to the finishing instructions on pages 125 to 128.

Quilt Layout

Shades of Blue Instructions

Approximate size: 65" x 77"
Block size: 12" finished
Approximate time: 12 hours

MATERIALS
³/₄ yd light blue
³/₄ yd medium light-blue
³/₄ yd medium blue
³/₄ yd dark blue
1 yd yellow
1 yd white
³/₄ yd first border fabric
¹/₂ yd second border fabric
1¹/₄ yds third border fabric
⁵/₈ yd binding fabric
3¹/₂ yds backing fabric
batting

CUTTING
Seven 3¹/₂"-wide strips, light blue
    Cut into forty 3¹/₂" x 6¹/₂" rectangles
Seven 3¹/₂"-wide strips, mediumlight-blue
    Cut into forty 3¹/₂" x 6¹/₂" rectangles
Seven 3¹/₂"-wide strips, medium blue
    Cut into forty 3¹/₂" x 6¹/₂" rectangles
Seven 3¹/₂"-wide strips, dark blue
    Cut into forty 3¹/₂" x 6¹/₂" rectangles
Eight 3¹/₂"-wide strips, yellow
    Cut into eighty 3¹/₂" x 3¹/₂" squares
Eight 3¹/₂"-wide strips, white
    Cut into eighty 3¹/₂" x 3¹/₂" squares
Six 3¹/₂"-wide strips, first border fabric
Eight 1¹/₂"-wide strips, second border
    fabric
Eight 5"-wide strips, third border fabric
Eight 2¹/₂"-wide strips, binding fabric

INSTRUCTIONS

Making the Block

1. Place white square right sides together with light blue rectangle; sew diagonally across white square. **Hint:** Draw a light pencil line diagonally on wrong side of white squares to provide a sewing guide.

2. Trim ¼" from sewing line and press resulting triangle open.

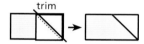

3. Repeat steps 1 and 2 for 20 of each of the following combinations of rectangles and squares.

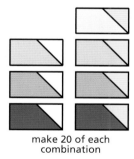

make 20 of each combination

4. Sew light blue/yellow rectangle to medium light-blue/yellow rectangle. Make 20.

5. Sew medium light-blue/white rectangle to medium blue/white rectangle. Make 20.

6. Sew dark blue/white rectangle to light blue/white rectangle. Make 20.

7. Sew dark blue/yellow rectangle to medium blue/yellow rectangle. Make 20.

8. Sew squares from steps 4 and 5 together. Press seams to one side.

(continued on next page)

9. Sew squares from steps 6 and 7 together. Press seams to opposite side.

10. Sew pairs of squares together to complete block.

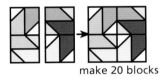

make 20 blocks

11. Make 20 blocks.

Making the Quilt Top

1. Place blocks in five rows of four blocks referring to layout. Sew blocks together in rows. Press seams for rows in alternating directions. Sew rows together. Press quilt top carefully.

2. Refer to Adding the Borders on page 125 to add three borders to your quilt top.

3. Complete your quilt referring to the finishing instructions on pages 125 to 128.

Quilt Layout

Log Cabin Garden Maze Instructions

Approximate size: 51" x 61"
Block size: 10" finished
Approximate time: 10 hours

MATERIALS

1/8 yd red print
7/8 yd beige/green print
1 1/8 yds green/purple paisley
1/2 yd dark red
1/2 yd first border fabric
1 1/8 yds second border fabric
5/8 yd binding fabric
3 1/2 yds backing fabric
batting

CUTTING

One 1 1/2"-wide strip, red print (center)
Ten 2 1/2"-wide strips, beige/green print
   (logs 1, 2, 9,10)
Fourteen 2 1/2"-wide strips, green/purple
   paisley (logs 3, 4, 11, 12)
Twelve 1"-wide strips, dark red (logs 5, 6,
   7, 8)
Six 2"-wide strips, first border fabric
Eight 4 1/2"-wide strips, second border
   fabric
Eight 2 1/2"-wide strips, binding fabric

INSTRUCTIONS

Making the Log Cabin Block

Log Cabin blocks are constructed by adding strips in numerical order to a center square. There are two different ways to add the strips.

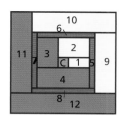

Method 1

1. Place beige/green strip right sides together with 1½"-wide red print strip and sew with ¼" seam allowance. Press seam toward beige/green print.

2. Cut strip set every 1½" for 20 center squares and log 1.

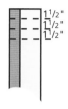

3. Take one pair from step 2 and turn clockwise; place beige/green strip right sides together along right edge and sew. Fold strip over, finger press and cut strip.

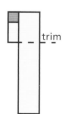
trim

4. Turn clockwise again and add green/purple paisley strip in same manner.

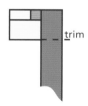
trim

5. Continue adding strips in order until block is complete. Make 20 Log Cabin blocks in same manner.

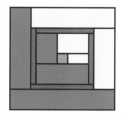

make 20 Log Cabin Blocks

(continued on next page)

Method 2

1. Cut strips in the following amounts:

center (red print):
    twenty 1½" x 1½"
log 1 (beige/green print):
    twenty 2½" x 1½" strips
log 2 (beige/green print):
    twenty 2½" x 3½" strips
log 3 (green/purple paisley):
    twenty 2½" x 3½" strips
log 4 (green/purple paisley):
    twenty 2½" x 5½"
log 5 (dark red):
    twenty 1" x 5½"
logs 6, 7 (dark red):
    forty 1" x 6"
log 8 (dark red):
    twenty 1" x 6½"
log 9 (beige/green print):
    twenty 2½" x 6½"
log 10 (beige/green print):
    twenty 2½" x 8½"
log 11 (green/purple paisley):
    twenty 2½" x 8½"
log 12 (green/purple paisley):
    twenty 2½" x 10½"

2. Sew log 1 to right edge of center square; finger press open.

3. Turn clockwise and sew log 2 to right edge; finger press open.

4. Turn clockwise and sew log 3 to right edge; finger press open.

5. Continue sewing logs in numerical order until block is complete. Make 20 Log Cabin blocks.

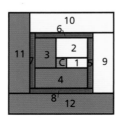

Making the Quilt Top

1. Place blocks in five rows of four blocks referring to layout. Sew blocks together in rows. Press seams for rows in alternating directions. Sew rows together. Press quilt top carefully.

2. Refer to Adding the Borders on page 125 to add first and second borders to your quilt top.

3. Complete your quilt referring to the finishing instructions on pages 125 to 128.

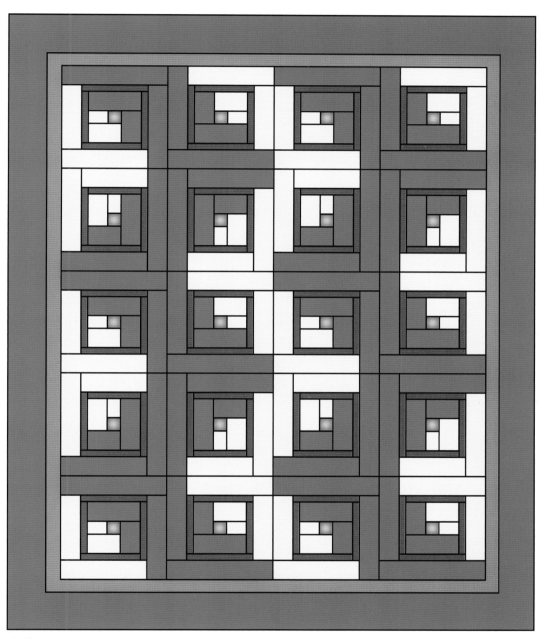

Quilt Layout

Fiery Zigzag Instructions

Approximate size: 48" x 60"
Block size: 6" finished
Approximate time: 8 hours

MATERIALS

1⅛ yds red
¾ yd yellow
¾ yd orange
½ yd first border fabric
1 yd second border fabric
⅝ yd binding fabric
3½ yds backing fabric
batting

CUTTING

Five 7"-wide strips, red
    Cut into 24 squares, 7" x 7"
Three 7¼"-wide strips, yellow
    Cut into 12 squares, 7¼" x 7¼"
Three 7¼"-wide strips, orange
    Cut into 12 squares, 7¼" x 7¼"
Six 2"-wide strips, first border fabric
Six 4½"-wide strips, second border
    fabric
Six 2½"-wide strips, binding fabric

INSTRUCTIONS

Making the Block

1. Cut red squares in half diagonally for 48 triangles.

2. Cut yellow and orange squares in quarters diagonally for 48 triangles.

3. Sew a yellow and orange triangle together. Press seam toward orange fabric. Make 24.

4. Repeat step 3 switching positions of yellow and orange triangles.

5. Sew a red triangle to each yellow/orange triangle to complete block.

6. Make 24 of each combination.

Making the Quilt Top

Note: Sew the quilt top in sections for easier handling.

1. For sections 1 and 3, place blocks in four rows of three blocks. Repeat.

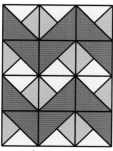

make 2 sections

2. For sections 2 and 4, place blocks in four rows of three blocks. Repeat.

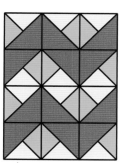

make 2 sections

3. Sew blocks together in rows. Press seams for rows in alternating directions. Sew rows together. Press sections carefully.

(continued on next page)

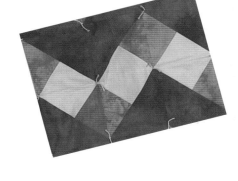

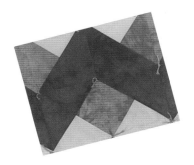

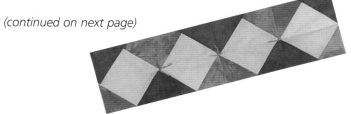

97

4. Sew sections 1 and 2 together. Repeat for sections 3 and 4.

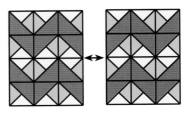

5. Sew sections together.

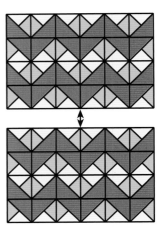

6. Refer to Adding the Borders on page 125 to add first and second borders to your quilt top.

7. Complete your quilt referring to the finishing instructions on pages 125 to 128.

Quilt Layout

Hug and Kiss Instructions

Approximate size: 57" x 57"
Block size: 12" finished
Approximate time: 10 hours

MATERIALS

⅞ yd light pink
⅞ yd light aqua
¾ yd white
½ yd turquoise
½ yd fuchsia
1 yd border fabric
⅝ yd binding fabric
3½ yds backing fabric
batting

CUTTING

Ten 2½"-wide strips, light pink
Ten 2½"-wide strips, light aqua
Four 5"-wide strips, white
   Cut into 32 squares, 5" x 5"
Two 5"-wide strips, turquoise
   Cut into 16 squares, 5" x 5"
Two 5"-wide strips, fuchsia
   Cut into 16 squares, 5" x 5"
Six 5"-wide strips, border fabric
Eight 2½"-wide strips, binding fabric

INSTRUCTIONS

Making Block A

1. Sew light aqua and light pink strip together. Make five strip sets. Press seams to one side.

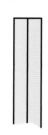

2. Cut strip sets every 2½" until you have 80 pairs of squares.

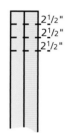

3. Sew pairs of squares to form a four patch. Make 40 four patches.

4. Draw a light pencil line diagonally across wrong side of white squares. Place a white square right sides together with a fuchsia square; sew ¼" from each side of drawn line.

5. Cut along drawn line to make two triangle squares. Make a total of 32 fuchsia/white triangle squares.

(continued on next page)

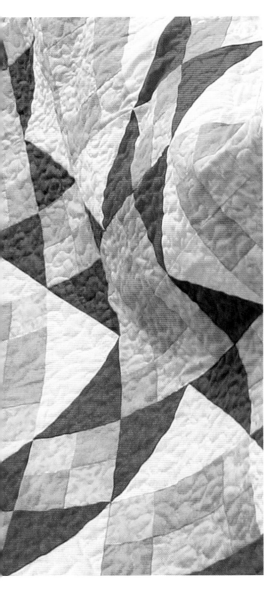

6. For rows 1 and 3, sew a four patch on opposite sides of a triangle square.

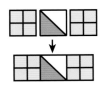

7. For row 2, sew a triangle square on opposite sides of a four patch.

8. Sew rows 1, 2 and 3 together to complete Block A. Make eight Block A.

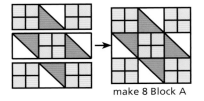

make 8 Block A

Making Block B

Substitute turquoise for fuchsia and repeat steps 1 through 8 in Making Block A to complete eight Block B.

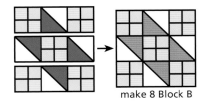

make 8 Block B

Making the Quilt Top

1. Place blocks in four rows of four blocks referring to layout. Sew blocks together in rows. Press seams for rows in alternating directions. Sew rows together. Press quilt top carefully.

2. Refer to Adding the Borders on page 125 to add border to your quilt top.

3. Complete your quilt referring to the finishing instructions on pages 125 to 128.

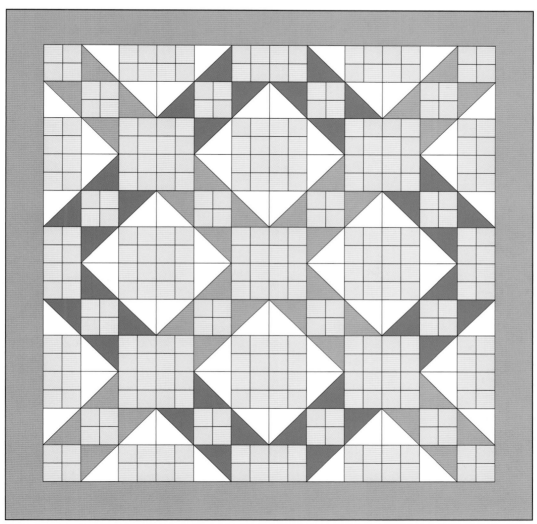

Quilt Layout

Oriental Garden Instructions

Approximate size: 54" x 66"
Block size: 6" finished
Approximate time: 7 hours

MATERIALS

$5/8$ yd floral print
$1/2$ yd light green
$1/2$ yd dark green
$3/4$ yd light pink
$3/4$ yd dark pink
$1/2$ yd first border fabric
1 yd second border fabric
$5/8$ yd binding fabric
$3^1/2$ yds backing fabric
batting

CUTTING

Three $6^1/2$"-wide strips, floral print
   Cut into twelve squares, $6^1/2$" x $6^1/2$"
Four $3^1/2$"-wide strips, light green
Four $3^1/2$"-wide strips, dark green
Six $3^1/2$"-wide strips, dark pink
Six $3^1/2$"-wide strips, light pink
Six 2"-wide strips, first border
Seven 4"-wide strips, second border
Seven $2^1/2$"-wide strips, binding

INSTRUCTIONS

Making Block A

1. Sew dark green and light green strips together. Press seams toward dark green.

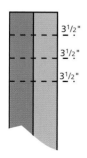

2. Cut strip sets every 3½" for 40 pairs of squares.

3. Sew pairs of squares together to complete Block A.

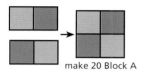

make 20 Block A

4. Make 20 Block A.

Making Block B

1. Sew light pink and dark pink strips together. Press seams toward dark pink.

2. Cut strip sets every 6½" to complete Block B.

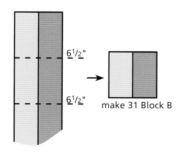

make 31 Block B

3. Make 31 Block B.

(continued on next page)

Quilt Layout

Making the Quilt Top

1. Place Blocks A and B and 6½" floral squares referring to the layout. Sew blocks together in rows. Press seams for rows in alternating directions. Sew rows together. Press quilt top carefully.

2. Refer to Adding the Borders on page 125 to add first and second borders to your quilt top.

3. Complete your quilt referring to the finishing instructions on pages 125 to 128.

Corner Stars Instructions

Approximate size: 49" x 49"

Block size: 4" finished

Approximate time: 8 hours

MATERIALS

$^7/_8$ yd dark green

$^5/_8$ yd light paisley

$^3/_8$ yd dark pink

$^3/_8$ yd dark gold

$^1/_2$ yd light pink

$^1/_2$ yd light gold

$^3/_8$ yd first border fabric

$^3/_4$ yd second border fabric

$^5/_8$ yd binding fabric

$3^1/_2$ yds backing fabric

batting

CUTTING

Five 5"-wide strips, dark green
  Cut into 34 squares, 5" x 5"
Three 5"-wide strips, light paisley
  Cut into 18 squares, 5" x 5"
One 5"-wide strip, dark pink
  Cut into eight squares, 5" x 5"
One 5"-wide strip, dark gold
  Cut into eight squares, 5" x 5"
Two 5"-wide strips, light pink
  Cut into 16 squares, 5" x 5"
Two 5"-wide strips, light gold
  Cut into 16 squares, 5" x 5"
Six 2"-wide strips, first border fabric
Six $3^1/_2$"-wide strips, second border fabric
Eight $2^1/_2$"-wide strips, binding fabric

INSTRUCTIONS

Making the Triangle Squares

1. Draw a light pencil line diagonally across the wrong sides of all light paisley, light gold and light pink squares.

2. Place light paisley and dark green squares right sides together; sew ¼" from each side of drawn line. Sew 18 pairs of squares.

3. Cut along drawn line for two triangle squares. Make 36 light paisley/dark green triangle squares.

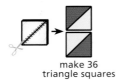

make 36
triangle squares

4. Repeat steps 2 and 3 with eight dark green and light pink squares, eight dark pink and light pink squares, eight light gold and dark green squares and eight light gold and dark gold squares.

make 16   make 16

make 16   make 16

5. Make 16 triangle squares of each color combination

Making the Quilt Top

Note: Make the quilt top in four sections, two with dark pink stars and two with dark gold stars.

1. For sections 1 and 4 (dark gold stars), place triangle squares in five rows of five triangle squares. Sew blocks together in rows. Press seams for rows in alternating directions. Sew rows together. Press carefully.

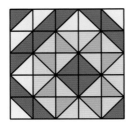

2. For sections 2 and 3 (dark pink stars), place triangle squares in five rows of five triangle squares. Sew blocks together in rows. Press seams for rows in alternating directions. Sew rows together. Press carefully.

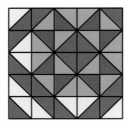

3. Sew sections 1 and 2 together; sew sections 3 and 4 together. Sew halves together.

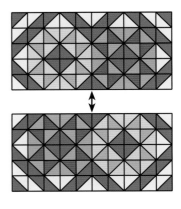

4. Refer to Adding the Borders on page 125 to add borders to your quilt top.

5. Complete your quilt referring to the finishing instructions on pages 125 to 128.

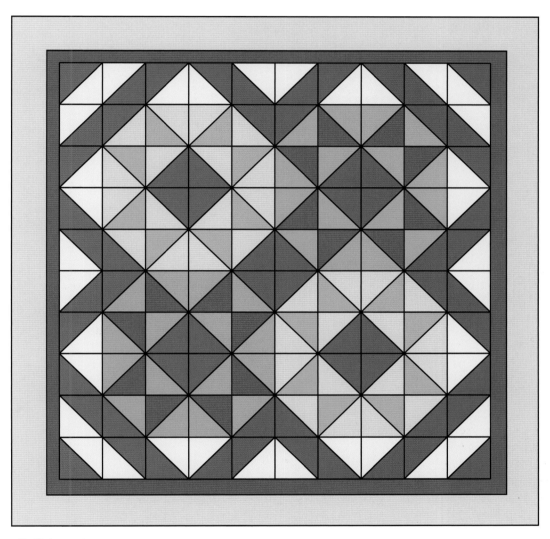

Quilt Layout

Mini Floral Appliqué Instructions

Approximate size: 24" x 24"
Block size: 11" finished
Approximate time: 3 hours

MATERIALS

Fat quarter each of green, white and
   floral print
*¹/₄–¹/₂ yd large floral print
³/₈ yd green (border)
³/₄ yd backing fabric
25" square batting
¹/₄ yd paper-backed fusible web
Invisible sewing thread
*Yardage of large floral print depends on
   size and number of individual floral
   motifs you will need for your mini quilt.

CUTTING

One 12" x 12" square, green
One 12" x 12" square, white
Two 10" x 10" squares, floral print
Three 3¹/₂"-wide strips, green border
   fabric

INSTRUCTIONS

1. Cut green, white and floral print squares in half diagonally.

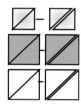

2. Sew a green and white triangle together to complete a triangle square; press seam toward green fabric.

3. Sew a floral print triangle to opposite sides of triangle square; press seam toward floral triangle.

4. Sew a floral print triangle to remaining sides; press seam toward floral print square.

5. Trim each side ¼" from point of green and white triangle.

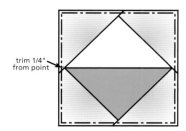

6. Prepare flowers for appliqué. Iron paper-backed fusible web to wrong side of large floral print following manufacturer's directions. Cut out desired number of flowers and leaves.

7. Remove paper backing, place flowers and leaves on triangle square in a pleasing arrangement. Fuse in place with iron following manufacturer's directions.

8. Cut piece of batting the same size as the quilt top. Pin together. Using invisible thread and a tiny zigzag stitch, sew around edges of all flowers and leaves. Using a straight stitch, sew in the ditch between triangle square and floral print triangles.

9. Measure quilt lengthwise; cut two border and batting strips to that length. Place batting strip on wrong side of border strip. Sew to side of quilt top. Repeat on opposite side.

10. Measure quilt crosswise; cut two border and batting strips to that length. Place batting strip on wrong side of border strip. Sew to top edge of quilt top. Repeat on bottom edge.

11. Cut backing fabric to equal measurements of quilt top. Place backing and quilt top right sides together. Sew along four sides using a ¼" seam allowance; leave an opening for turning.

12. Turn quilt right side out; whip-stitch opening closed.

13. Topstitch ¼" from edge of quilt.

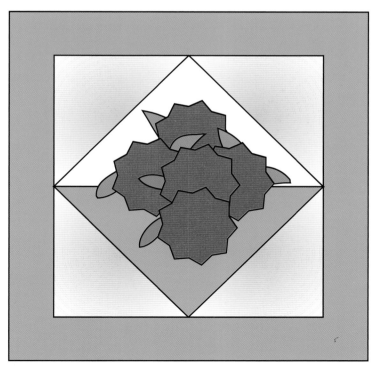

Quilt Layout

111

Animal Checkerboard Instructions

Approximate size: 51" x 51"
Block size: 9" finished
Approximate time: 7 hours

MATERIALS
1 yd yellow
1¼ yds pink
1–1½ yds animal print 1
1 yd animal print 2
½ yd binding fabric
2½ yds backing fabric
batting

CUTTING
Eight 3½"-wide strips, yellow
Eleven 3½"-wide strips, pink
  Cut four strips into 40 squares,
  3½" x 3½"
Ten 9½" squares, animal print 1
Two 9½" x 27½" rectangles,
  animal print 2
Four 3½" corner squares, yellow
Six 2½"-wide strips, binding fabric

INSTRUCTIONS

Making the Nine Patch Blocks

1. Sew a yellow strip to each side of a pink strip. Press seams toward pink print.

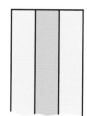

2. Cut strip set every 3½" for rows 1 and 3.

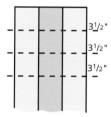

3. Sew a pink strip to each side of a yellow strip. Press seams toward pink print.

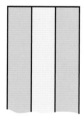

4. Cut strip set every 3½" for row 2.

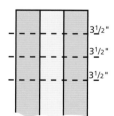

5. Sew rows 1, 2 and 3 together to complete Nine Patch.

6. Make nine Nine Patch blocks.

Making the Alternate Blocks

1. Place pink square right sides together with 9½" animal print 1 square; sew diagonally across pink square. **Hint:** Draw a light pencil line diagonally on wrong side of pink squares to provide a sewing guide.

2. Trim ¼" from sewing line and press resulting triangle open.

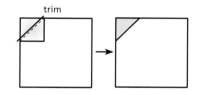

3. Repeat steps 1 and 2 on remaining three corners of animal print 1 squares .

4. Repeat steps 1, 2 and 3 for a total of ten Alternate blocks.

Making the Quilt

1. Place Nine Patch blocks, Alternate blocks and 9½" x 27½" animal print 2 rectangles according to quilt layout.

2. Sew blocks for first row together. Repeat for last row.

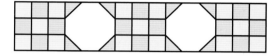

3. Sew an Alternate block to top and bottom edge of a Nine Patch block. Repeat two more times. Sew block rows together with the 9½" x 27½" rows in between for middle section.

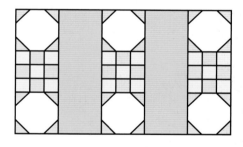

4. Sew first and last row to middle section.

5. For border, sew a yellow strip to each side of a pink strip for Strip 1; cut at 3½" intervals. Sew a pink strip to each side of a yellow strip for Strip 2; cut at 3½" intervals.

(continued on next page)

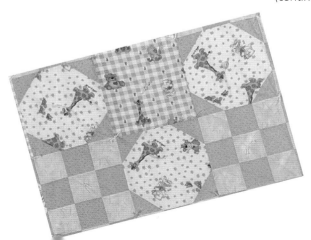

6. For each border strip, sew three Strip 2 and two Strip 1 together; repeat).

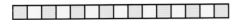

7. Sew a pieced border strip to sides of quilt.

8. Sew a 3¹/₂" yellow square to opposite ends of remaining two pieced borders. Sew to top and bottom of quilt.

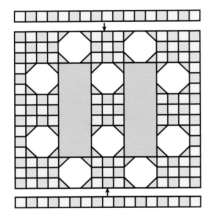

9. Complete your quilt referring to the finishing instructions on pages 125 to 128. Photographed quilt was tied using 100% cotton yarn (see Tying the Quilt, page 126).

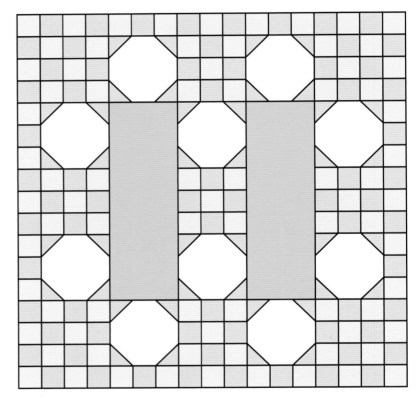

Quilt Layout

Log Cabin Appliqué Instructions

Approximate size: 38" x 38"
Block size: 8" finished
Approximate time: 7 hours

MATERIALS
³/₈ yd red
fat quarter gold
⁷/₈ yd medium green
¹/₂ yd medium blue
¹/₂ yd light green
¹/₂ yd light blue
1¹/₄ yds backing
1¹/₂ yds batting
1 yd paper-backed fusible web
Invisible thread

CUTTING
Eight 7" squares, light blue
Eight 7" squares, light green
Sixteen 2¹/₂" x 6¹/₂" strips, medium green
Sixteen 2¹/₂" x 8¹/₂" strips, medium blue
Four 3¹/₂"-wide strips, medium green
   (border)
Four 3¹/₂" squares, medium blue
   (corner squares)
Sixteen 8¹/₂" squares, batting
Two 3¹/₂" x 32¹/₂" strips, batting
Two 3¹/₂" x 38¹/₂" strips, batting

INSTRUCTIONS

Making the Blocks

1. Cut the 7" light green and light blue squares in half diagonally.

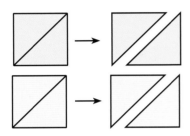

2. Sew a light blue triangle to a light green triangle making a triangle square. Press seam to one side. Make a total of 16 triangle squares.

3. Trim triangle squares to 6½".

4. Trace 16 Flowers, 16 Flower Centers and 16 Leaves onto paper side of fusible web. Place fusible web on wrong side of corresponding fabric – red for flowers, gold for flower centers and medium green for leaves; iron to fuse following manufacturer's instructions.

5. Cut out shapes and place on triangle squares; fuse in place.

6. Sew a 2½" x 6½" medium green strip to triangle square; press seam toward medium green strip.

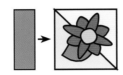

7. Sew a 2½" x 6½" medium blue strip to adjacent side to complete block; press seam toward medium blue strip.

8. Place a batting square on wrong side of block; pin together if desired. Using invisible thread and a tiny zigzag, sew around edges of flower, center and leaf.

9. Using a straight stitch, sew in the ditch between triangle square and medium green and medium blue strips.

10. Repeat steps 6 to 9 for remaining blocks. You will have 16 already-quilted blocks.

Making the Quilt Top

1. Place blocks in four rows of four blocks. Sew the blocks together in pairs, then sew the pairs together. Continue sewing until all blocks are sewn together. Remember to press seams for rows in alternating directions.

2. Measure length and width of quilt. Cut and sew four border strips to equal the length and width measurements.

3. Place a 3½" x 32½" batting strip on wrong side of a border strip; sew to side of quilt. Repeat on the opposite side.

4. Sew a medium blue square to opposite ends of remaining medium green border strips. Place a 3½" x 38½" batting strip on wrong side of a border strip; sew to top of quilt. Repeat on bottom edge.

5. Cut backing fabric to equal measurements of quilt top. Place backing right sides together with quilt top. Sew along all four sides using a ¼" seam allowance; leave an opening for turning.

6. Turn quilt right side out; whip-stitch opening closed.

7. Topstitch ¼" from edge of quilt.

Quilt Layout

Flower Center

Leaf

Flower

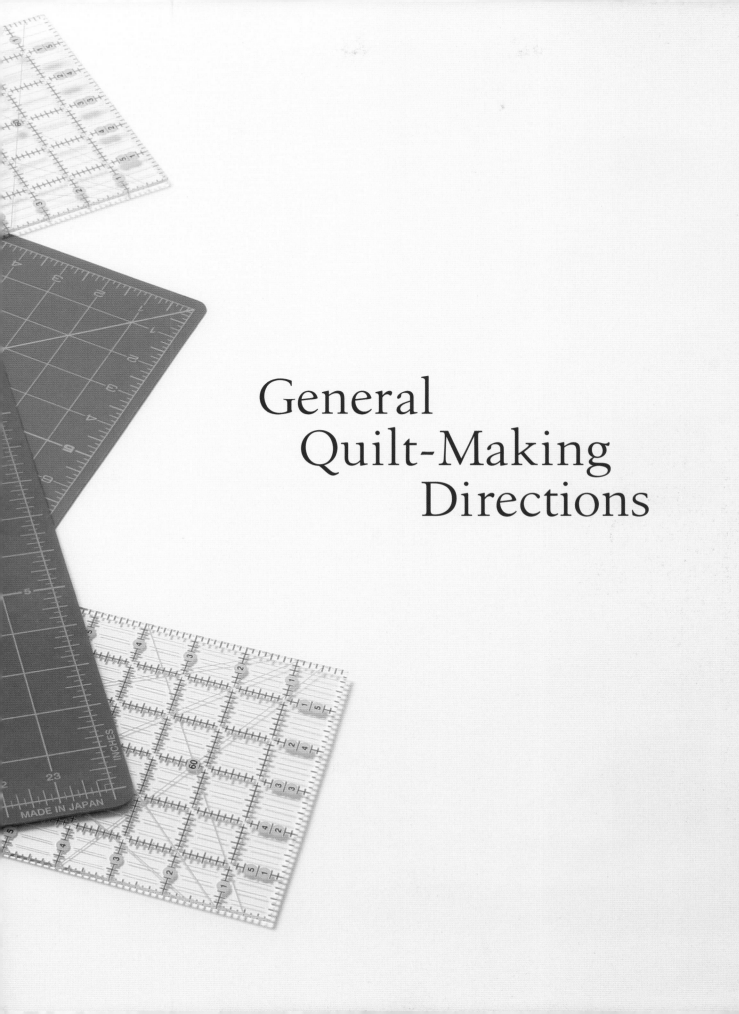

General
Quilt-Making
Directions

General Directions

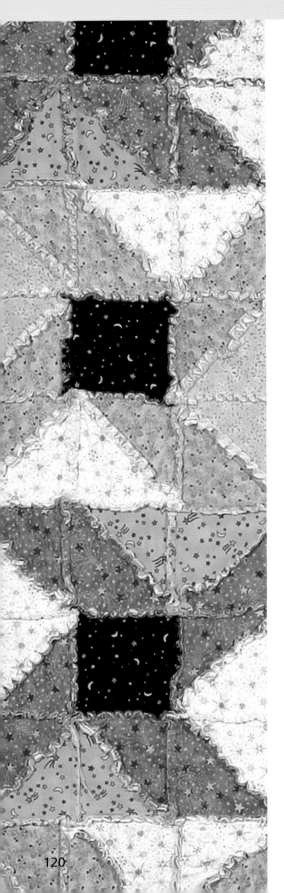

In order to make a quilt in 24 hours you will need to follow some fast quilt-making techniques that are discussed in this section. Of course, if you prefer, you can use traditional methods. But, keep in mind, your quilt will probably take more than 24 hours.

FABRIC

For several hundred years, quilts were made with 100% cotton fabric, and this remains today the fabric of choice for most quilters.

There are many properties in cotton that make it especially well-suited to quilt-making. There is less distortion in cotton fabric, thereby affording the quilter greater security in making certain that even the smallest bits of fabric will fit together. Because a quilt block made of cotton can be ironed flat with a steam iron, a puckered area, created by mistake, can be fixed. The sewing machine needle can move through cotton with a great deal of ease when compared to some synthetic fabrics. While you may find that quilt artists today often use other kinds of fabric, to create these quilts quickly and accurately, 100% cotton is strongly recommended.

Cotton fabric today is produced in so many wonderful and exciting combinations of prints and solids that it is often difficult to pick colors for your quilt. We've chosen our favorite colors for these quilts, but don't be afraid to make your own choices. To get ideas for color combinations, look at pictures of quilts that you like. Visit quilt shows and museums. If you find a quilt that appeals to you, try using similar colors in your quilt. Sometimes a favorite painting or a piece of fabric may give you an idea for a color combination.

For years, quilters were advised to prewash all of their fabric to test for colorfastness and shrinkage. Now most quilters don't bother to prewash all of their fabric, but they do *pretest* it. Cut a strip about 2" wide from each piece of fabric that you will use in your quilt. Measure both the length and the width of the strip. Then immerse it in a bowl of very hot water, using a separate bowl for each piece of fabric. Be especially concerned about reds and dark blues because they have a tendency to bleed if the initial dyeing was not done correctly. If it's one of your favorite fabrics that's bleeding, you might be able to salvage the fabric. Try washing the fabric in very hot water until you've washed out all of the excess dye. Unfortunately, fabrics that continue to bleed after they have been washed repeatedly will bleed forever. So, eliminate them right at the start.

Now, take each one of the strips and iron them dry with a hot iron. Be especially careful not to stretch the strip. When the strips are completely dry, measure and compare them to your original strip. If all of your fabric is shrinking the same amount, you don't have to worry about uneven shrinkage in your quilt. When you wash the final quilt, the puckering that will result will give you the look of an antique quilt. If you don't want this look, you are going to have to wash and dry all of your fabric before you start cutting. Iron the fabric, using some spray starch or sizing to give the fabric a crisp finish.

If you are never planning to wash your quilt, i.e. your quilt is intended to be a wall hanging, you could eliminate the pre-testing process. You may run the risk, however, of some future relative to whom you have willed your quilts deciding that the wall hanging needs freshening by washing.

Before beginning to work, make sure that your fabric is absolutely square. If it is not, you will have difficulty cutting square pieces. Fabric is woven with crosswise and lengthwise threads. Lengthwise threads should be parallel to the selvage (that's the finished edge along the sides; sometimes the fabric company prints its name along the selvage), and crosswise threads should be perpendicular to the selvage. If fabric is off grain, you can usually straighten it by pulling gently on the true bias in the opposite direction to the off-grain edge. Continue doing this until the crosswise threads are at a right angle to the lengthwise threads.

ROTARY CUTTING

The introduction of the rotary cutter in the late 1970s has made all the difference in quilt making today. None of the quilts in this book could have been completed in 24 hours with the traditional template technique; however, with rotary cutting you can make quilts faster and with greater accuracy. With rotary cutting, traditional quilt templates are not used. Instead, the pieces are cut into strips and then the strips are cut into other shapes.

For rotary cutting, you will need three important tools: a rotary cutter, a mat and an acrylic ruler. There are currently on the market many different brands and

types. Choose the kinds that you feel will work for you. Ask your quilting friends what their preferences are, then make your decision.

There are several different rotary cutters now available with special features that you might prefer, such as the type of handle, whether the cutter can be used for both right- and left-handed quilters, safety features, size, and finally the cost.

Don't attempt to use the rotary cutter without an accompanying protective mat. The mat will not only protect your table from becoming scratched, but it will protect your cutter as well. The mat is self-healing and will not dull the cutting blades. Mats are available in many sizes, but if this is your first attempt at rotary cutting, an 18" x 24" mat is probably your best choice. When you are not using your mat, be sure that it is sitting on a flat surface. Otherwise your mat will bend. If you want to keep your mat from warping, make certain that it is not sitting in direct sunlight; the heat can cause the mat to warp. You won't be able to get accurate cutting when you use a bent or warped mat.

A must for cutting accurate strips is a strong straight edge. Acrylic rulers are the perfect choice for this. There are many different acrylic rulers on the market, and they come in several widths and lengths. Either a 6" x 24" or a 6" x 12" ruler will be the most useful. The longer ruler will allow you to fold your fabric only once while the smaller size will require folding the fabric twice. Make sure that your ruler has $1/8$" increment markings in both directions plus a 45-degree marking.

CUTTING STRIPS

Before beginning to work, iron your fabric to remove the wrinkles. Fold the fabric in half, lengthwise, bringing the selvedge edges together. Fold in half again. Make sure that there are no wrinkles in the fabric.

Now place the folded fabric on the cutting mat. Place the fabric length on the right side if you are right-handed or on the left side if you are left-handed. The fold of the fabric should line up along one of the grid lines printed on the mat.

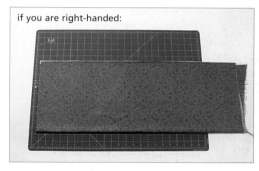

if you are right-handed:

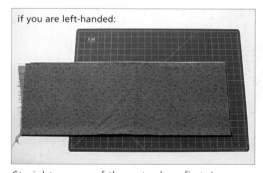

if you are left-handed:

Straighten one of the cut edges first. Lay the acrylic ruler on the mat near the cut edge; the ruler markings should be even with the grid on the mat. Hold the ruler firmly with your left hand (or, with your right hand if you are left-handed). To provide extra stability, keep your small finger off the mat. Now hold the rotary cutter

with the blade against the ruler and cut away from you in one quick motion.

Carefully turn fabric (or mat with fabric) so straightened edge is on opposite side. Place the ruler on the required width line along the cut edge of the fabric and cut the strip, making sure that you always cut away from you. Cut the number of strips called for in the directions.

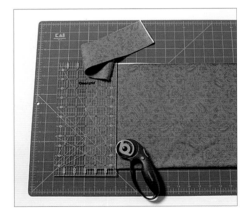

After you have cut a few strips, you will want to check to make certain that your fabric continues to be perfectly square. If necessary, you should re-square the fabric. If you fail to do this, your strips may

be bowed with a "v" in the center, causing your piecing to become inaccurate as you continue working.

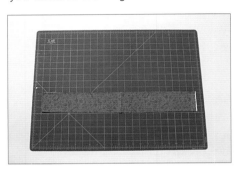

CUTTING SQUARES AND RECTANGLES
Place a stack of strips on the cutting mat. You will be more successful in cutting – at least in the beginning – if you work with no more than four strips at a time. Make certain that the strips are lined up very evenly. Following the instructions given for the quilt, cut the required number of squares or rectangles.

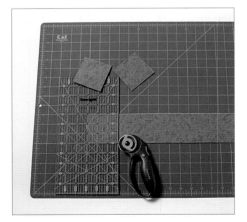

CUTTING TRIANGLES

There are a number of different triangle constructions used in these quilts including Half-Square Triangles, Quarter-Square Triangles, and Triangle Squares.

The short sides of a Half-Square Triangle are on the straight grain of the fabric. This is especially necessary if the short edges are on the outer side of the block. Cut the squares the size indicated in the instructions, then cut the square in half diagonally.

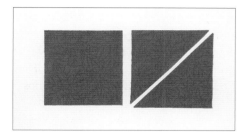

Quarter-Square Triangles are used when the long edge of the triangle must be on the straight grain. This is important when the long edge is on the outside edge of the block. Again, cut the squares the proper size; then cut diagonally into quarters.

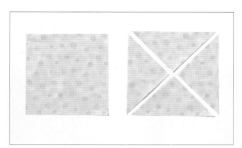

Triangle Squares are squares made up of two different-colored triangles. To make these squares, you can cut individual triangles as described in Half-Square Triangles. Then sew two triangles together. A quick method, especially if you have several triangle squares with the same fabric, is to sew two squares together. Then draw a diagonal line on the wrong side of the lighter square. Place two squares right sides together and sew ¼" from each side of the drawn line.

Cut along the drawn line, and you have created two Triangle Squares.

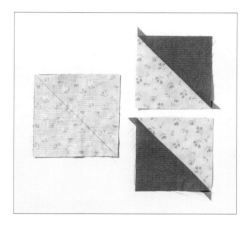

STITCH AND FLIP

This is a method for quickly creating triangles and octagons or trapezoids. Instead of cutting these shapes, you cut and sew squares or rectangles together.

With right sides together, a small square is placed in the corner of a larger square or rectangle. You then sew diagonally from corner to corner of the small square.

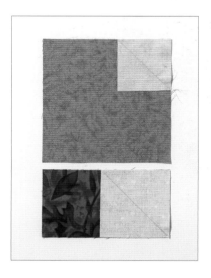

Trim the corner about ¹/₄" from the seam line.

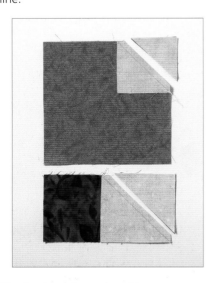

Flip the triangle over and iron.

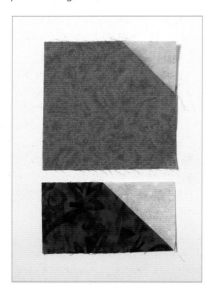

Repeat at the other corners *according to individual pattern instructions.*

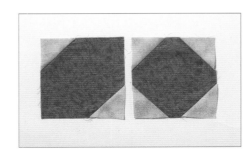

STRIP PIECING

Most of the quilts in this book are done using the strip-piecing technique. This is a much faster and easier method of making quilts rather than creating the blocks piece by piece. With this method, two or more strips are sewn together then cut at certain intervals. For instance, if a block is made up of several 3" finished squares, cut 3¹/₂"-wide strips along the crosswise grain.

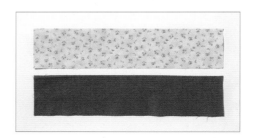

With right sides together, sew two strips along the length. The seam should be pressed toward the dark side of the fabric.

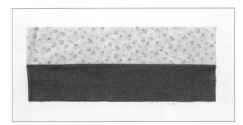

Cut across strips at 3¹/₂" intervals to create pairs of 3¹/₂" squares.

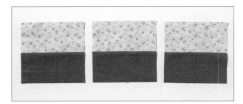

CHAIN PIECING

Another quick technique to enable you to finish these quilts in 24 hours (or less!) is chain piecing. This technique is used when there are several of the same shape to sew together. If you want to sew several triangles together, place the first two with their right sides together and sew along the longest edge. Do not begin and end your thread with each triangle, but let the thread run over a continuous chain of triangles. When you have made a row of triangles, snip them apart. Don't worry about the threads coming undone; they will eventually be anchored by the cross seams.

SEWING THE BLOCKS TOGETHER

Make the number of blocks as stated in the individual pattern instructions. You can sew the blocks together in pairs and then sew pairs together. Continue sewing in pairs until all blocks are sewn together. Another way to sew blocks together is to sew them in rows, then sew rows together. Whichever method you choose, be sure to press seams of adjoining rows in opposite directions.

ADDING BORDERS

Borders are usually added to the top, sides and bottom of a quilt.

To add your borders, measure the quilt top lengthwise and cut two border strips to that length by the width measurement given in the instructions. Strips may have to be pieced to achieve the correct length. Sew both strips to the sides of the quilt. Now measure the quilt top crosswise, being sure to include the borders you have just added. Cut two border strips, following the width measurement given in the instructions.

Add these borders to the top and bottom of the quilt. Repeat this process for any additional borders. Use the 1/4" seam allowance at all times and press all of the seams to the darker side. Press the quilt top carefully.

ATTACHING THE BATTING AND BACKING

There are a number of different types of batting on the market today including the new fusible battings that eliminate the need for basting. Your choice of batting will depend upon how you are planning to use your quilt. If your quilt is to serve as a wall hanging, you will probably want to use a thin cotton batting.

Batting made with a thin cotton or cotton/polyester blend works best for machine quilting. Very thick polyester batting should be used only for tied quilts.

The best fabric for quilt backing is 100% cotton fabric. If your quilt is larger than the available fabric, you will have to piece your backing fabric. When joining the fabric, try not to have a seam going down the center. Instead cut off the selvages and make a center strip that is about 36" wide and have narrower strips at the sides. Seam the pieces together and carefully iron the seams open. (This is the one of the few times in making a quilt that a seam should be pressed open.) Several fabric manufacturers are now selling 90" or 108"-wide fabrics for use as backing.

The batting and the backing should be cut about one to two inches larger on all sides than the quilt top. Place the backing wrong side up on a flat surface. Smooth out the batting on top of this, matching the outer edges. Center the quilt top, right side up, on top of the batting.

Now the quilt layers must be held together before quilting, and there are several methods for doing this:

Thread Basting: Baste the three layers together with long stitches. Start in the center and sew toward the edges in a number of diagonal lines.

Safety-pin Basting: Starting from the center and working toward the edges, pin through all layers at one time with large safety pins. The pins should be placed no more than 4"

apart. As you work, think of your quilting plan to make sure that the pins will avoid prospective quilting lines.

Quilt-gun Basting: This handy trigger tool pushes nylon tags through all layers of the quilt. Start in the center and work toward the outside edges. The tags should be placed about 4" apart. You can sew right over the tags, which can then be easily removed by cutting them off with scissors.

Spray or Heat-set Basting: Several manufacturers have spray adhesives available especially for quilters. Apply these products by following the manufacturers' directions. You might want to test these products before you use them to make sure that they meet with your requirements.

Fusible Iron-on Batting: These battings are a wonderful new way to hold quilt layers together without using any of the other time-consuming methods of basting. Again, you will want to test these battings to be certain that you are happy with the results. Follow the manufacturers' directions.

QUILTING

If you like the process of hand quilting, you can – of course – finish these projects by hand quilting. However, if you want to finish these quilts in 24 hours, you will have to use a sewing machine for quilting.

If you have never used a sewing machine for quilting, you may want to find a book and read about the technique. You

do not need a special machine for quilting. Just make sure that your machine has been oiled and is in good working condition.

If you are going to do machine quilting, you should invest in an even-feed foot. This foot is designed to feed the top and bottom layers of a quilt evenly through the machine. The foot prevents puckers from forming as you machine quilt. Use a fine transparent nylon thread in the top and regular sewing thread in the bobbin.

"Quilting in the Ditch" is one of the easiest ways to machine quilt. This is a term used to describe stitching in the space between two pieces of fabric that have been sewn together. Using your fingers, pull the blocks or pieces apart slightly and machine stitch right between the two pieces. The stitching will look better if you keep the stitching to the side of the seam that does not have the extra bulk of the seam allowance under it. The quilting will be hidden in the seam.

Free-Form machine quilting can be used to quilt around a design, to quilt a motif, or to quilt an overall pattern. The quilting is done with a darning foot and the feed dogs down on the sewing machine. It takes practice to master Free-Form quilting because you are controlling the movement of the quilt under the needle rather than the sewing machine moving the quilt. You can quilt in any direction: up and down, side to side-even in circles—without pivoting the quilt around the needle. Before you try to do Free-Form quilting on your quilt, you should practice first.

TYING THE QUILT

An easy way to finish a quilt is to "tie" it. Use embroidery floss, pearl cotton, yarn or other washable material.

Thread an 18" length of tying material into a large tapestry needle. (Curved quilters' needles also work well.) Do not knot the thread!

It's a good idea to work from the center of the quilt out, adjusting any excess fullness. Take the needle down from the top through all three layers, leaving a short tail on the right side. Bring the needle back up a short distance away. Go back down through the original hole and up through the second hole. Tie the ends of the yarn into a double knot and trim to 1". Repeat knots at corners and random areas of the blocks. If you don't want the loose ends on the front of your quilt, repeat the above steps except start from the back and tie knots on the back of the quilt.

ATTACHING THE CONTINUOUS MACHINE BINDING

Once the quilt has been quilted or tied, the edges must be bound. While again this can be done by hand, in order to finish your quilt in 24 hours, this process needs to be done on the sewing machine.

Start by trimming the backing and batting even with the quilt top. Measure the quilt top and cut enough 2½"-wide strips to go around all four sides of the quilt plus 6". Join the strips end to end with diagonal seams and trim the corners.

Press the seams open. Cut one end of the strip at a 45-degree angle and press under ¼".

Press entire strip in half lengthwise, wrong sides together.

On the back of the quilt, position the binding in the middle of one side, keeping the raw edges together. Sew the binding to the quilt with the ¼" seam allowance, beginning about an inch below the folded end of the binding.

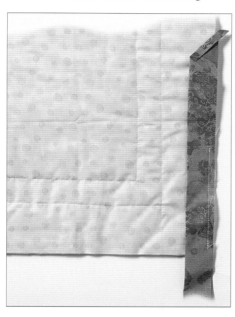

At the corner, stop ¼" from the edge of the quilt and backstitch.

Fold binding away from the quilt so it is at a right angle to edge just sewn. Then, fold the binding back on itself so the fold is on the quilt edge and the raw edges are aligned with the adjacent side of the quilt. Begin sewing at the quilt edge.

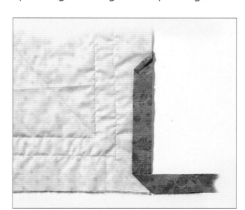

Continue in the same way around the remaining sides of the quilt. Stop about two inches away from the starting point. Trim any excess binding and tuck it inside the folded end. Finish the stitching.

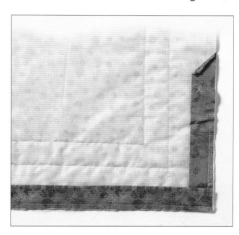

Fold the binding to the front of the quilt so the seam line is covered; use the small zigzag stitch and invisible thread on the top of the machine and sew along entire edge of binding. The bobbin should have matching thread.

PILLOWCASE FINISHING

For a really quick method to completing a quilt, try "pillowcase finishing." After you have completed your quilt top, place the batting on a flat surface. Smooth out the backing, right side up on top of the batting. Place the quilt top, right sides together with the backing. Pin or baste the three layers together. Sew along all four edges with a 1/4" seam allowance, leaving an opening on one side for turning. Turn the quilt right side out, and stitch the opening closed. Top stitch 1/4" from the outside edge of the quilt. Quilt by machine or use ties to finish your quilt.

FINISHING TOUCHES

If your quilt is to be a wall hanging you will need to add a sleeve to the back. Measure your quilt across the width. Cut a strip of fabric to that length and about 6" wide. Fold short ends 1/2" toward wrong side, then fold another 1/2". Sew along first fold. Fold strip in half lengthwise with wrong sides together. Sew with a 1/4" seam allowance. Press seam allowance open turning strip so seam is down the center. Place sewn strip on back of quilt along top edge with seam side down and carefully whip stitch along bottom and top edge of sleeve.

After you have finished making your quilt, always sign and date it. You can make a label by cross stitching or embroidering or even writing on a label or on the back of your quilt with a permanent marking pen. If you are friends with your computer, you can even create an attractive label on the computer.

SPECIAL TECHNIQUES

Machine Appliqué

Appliqué is often thought by many to be something they would like to do but not something that they are able to do. But, by using large floral prints or simple patterns, paper-backed fusible web and

machine stitching, appliqué is now easier than ever.

If you are using appliqué patterns (see Log Cabin Appliqué, page 115), trace the number of pattern shapes needed for your quilt onto the paper side of fusible web. Iron the fusible web to the wrong side of the fabric following the manufacturer's directions. Cut out pattern pieces along drawn lines.

If you are using a large floral print (see Mini Floral Appliqué, page 110), iron paper-backed fusible web to wrong side of fabric. Cut out the number of flowers and leaves needed for your project.

Peel off paper from back of fabric shapes and position on background fabric or block. Iron in place following manufacturer's directions. Appliqué around all outer edges of floral shapes using a small machine zigzag and invisible nylon thread in your sewing machine.

Quilting as You Appliqué

Your appliquéd quilt top can be made even quicker if you quilt as you appliqué. Before machine zigzagging around the shapes, place block on top of a piece of thin cotton batting that is cut the same size. Machine appliqué around shapes using a small zigzag stitch and invisible nylon thread in your machine. Finish your quilt according to individual pattern instructions.

FUSSY CUTTING

A timesaving technique that was used in some of the quilts is the use of fabric squares that are fussy cut instead of blocks that are pieced. Novelty prints and large florals are perfect for fussy cutting

(see Oriental Garden, page 104 and Angel Fantasy, page 56).

Unfold your fabric and spread out on a table with your cutting mat under the area you will be cutting first. Use a piece of clear template plastic cut to the dimensions needed for your quilt. Place plastic on top of fabric, moving it until you have the motif centered in the area under the plastic square. Using a marking pencil, trace around square. Cut out using a rotary cutter (or scissors). Continue moving plastic around fabric, tracing and cutting out motifs until you have the necessary number of fabric squares for your quilt. Be sure to have the cutting mat under your fabric if rotary cutting.

Timesaving Hint: A 12 1/2" square acrylic ruler is very useful when fussy cutting. Use masking tape to mark the lines for the dimensions of the square needed for your quilt. Move ruler around until in desired position and cut out with your rotary cutter. Be sure cutting mat is in place.